HOW TO BE AN ALIEN

It's easy

IN
- BRITAIN
- FRANCE
- ITALY
- GERMANY
- SWITZERLAND
- ISRAEL
- JAPAN

DRAWINGS BY *Nicolas Bentley & David Langdon*

BASIC BOOKS, INC., PUBLISHERS

NEW YORK

Library of Congress Catalog Card Number: 64-13196

Manufactured in the United States of America

DESIGNED BY VINCENT TORRE

PREFACE

I am an experienced beginner, a middle-aged young writer, an unpublished best seller. All this as far as America is concerned.

My relationship with the United States used to puzzle me. Why was it, I asked myself, that my books were, for better or worse, published in twenty-three languages, sold reasonably well almost all over the world, but, apart from some small exceptions hardly worth mentioning, were totally and uncompromisingly rejected by American publishers? Then I believed that I had found the answer: because American publishers were more intelligent and less gullible than others; they had seen through me. Whatever my faults may be, I am not a man of wild conceit. I do not hold myself in particularly high esteem either as a man or as a writer, and I do not revere myself with that breathless admiration I often see—and sometimes envy—in many of my colleagues. I was driven to the conclusion that, though my writings may have fooled others, American publishers had better judgment and clearer insight than publishers all over the world.

Then, many years ago, the third phase followed, and my lack of self-confidence was shaken. Perhaps my modesty was not built on firm enough foundations; perhaps I always cherished a secret fondness for myself. Be that as it may, I was slowly driven to the conclusion that my writings were wortly of some notice and that American publishers were fools.

At first, this was nothing more than a vague conjecture. Here is an author—I mused—one of whose books sold 300,000 and another over 100,000 in hard covers in England; who became a best seller in quite a few countries; whose books are conspicuously displayed in innumerable shop windows and book stores all over Europe, Australia, Africa, and South America. Considering how much rubbish U.S. publishers print, why doesn't one of their number try his luck with this guy, just for the hell of it? If the book is a flop, well, it won't be the first—or the last—time his publishing house has missed out, but there is *some* evidence, at least, that it might not be. Thus I spake in the name of that publisher; but no publisher spake in similar vein, and they all left me untouched.

My suspicion that the American publisher is slightly dim increased when I learned that large numbers of *the English editions* of my books found their way to American readers and, believe it or not, quite a few of these readers found them acceptable, even mildly amusing.

Finally, my suspicions about American publishers turned into firm and unshakable conviction when I reread their innumerable letters of rejection. A few did not like my work, and that is fair enough. But—and this is really peculiar—most loved it. I have hardly ever read such fulsome, breathless adulation of myself than in these letters of rejection written by American publishers. They had, they asserted, hardly ever been so capitally amused. They thought the world of me. But, alas, their public was not half so sophisticated and intelligent as they were themselves, so, with bleeding hearts, they very much regretted, etc., etc.

Many said that I was too high-brow. T. S. Eliot was not too high-brow; Robert Graves was not too high-brow; I was. Then, for a few dozen, I was too English. Graham Greene was not too English; Winston Churchill was not too English; but I—a refugee from Central Europe—was much too English to bear. And so on, and so on.

I often felt that this great nation deserved better publishers than it had. At the same time, I shrugged my shoulders and resigned myself to my fate. The United States of America and I, I thought, will just have to learn to live without each other. And we did. In fact, both of us prospered in our own modest ways.

Then, one day, I met that unusual and unexpected phenomenon which I had thought extinct: an American editor who knew true gold when he saw it. He declared himself prepared to take the risk of introducing me to the American public and print an anthology of my work. Here is the result.

I wish his firm the very, very good luck that its courage and superlative judgment deserve.

And you, America, brace yourself! This may well be your last chance.

G.M.

London
January 1964

CONTENTS

HOW TO BE AN ALIEN

I

√ BRITAIN
FRANCE
ITALY
GERMANY
SWITZERLAND
ISRAEL
JAPAN

ONCE A FOREIGNER . . .

I believe, without undue modesty, that I have certain qualifications to write on "how to be an alien." I am an alien myself. What is more, I have been an alien all my life. Only, during the first twenty-six years of my life I was not aware of this plain fact. I was living in my own country, a country full of aliens, and I noticed nothing particular or irregular about myself; then I came to England, and you can imagine my painful surprise.

Like all great and important discoveries, it was a matter of a few seconds. You probably all know from your school days how Isaac Newton discovered the law of gravity. An apple fell on his head. This incident set him thinking for a minute or two. Then he exclaimed joyfully: "Of course! The gravitation constant is the acceleration per second that a mass of one gram causes at a distance of one centimeter." You were also taught that James Watt one day went into the kitchen where cabbage was cooking and saw the lid of the saucepan rise and fall. "Now let me think," he murmured—"let me think." Then he struck his forehead, and the steam engine was discovered. It was the same with me, although circumstances were rather different.

It was like this. Some years ago, I spent a lot of time with a young lady who was very proud and conscious of being English. Once she asked me—to my great surprise—whether I would marry her. "No," I replied, "I will not. My mother would never agree to my marrying a foreigner." She looked at me, a little surprised and irritated, and retorted: "I, a foreigner? What a silly thing to say. I am English. You are the foreigner. And your mother, too." I did not give in. "In Budapest, too?" I asked her. "Everywhere," she declared with determination. "Truth does not depend on geography. What is true in England is also true in Hungary and in North Borneo and Venezuela and everywhere."

I saw that this theory was as irrefutable as it was simple. I was startled and upset, mainly because of my mother, whom I loved and respected. Now, I suddenly learned what she really was.

It was a shame and bad taste to be an alien, and it is no use pretending otherwise. There is no way out of it. A criminal may improve and become a decent member of society. A foreigner cannot improve. Once a foreigner, always a foreigner. There is no way out for him. He may become British; he can never become English.

So it is better to reconcile yourself to the sorrowful reality. There are some noble English people who might forgive you. There are some magnanimous souls who realize that it is not your fault, only your misfortune. They will treat you with condescension, understanding, and sympathy. They will invite you to their homes. Just as they keep lap dogs and other pets, they are quite prepared to keep a few foreigners.

The title of this book consequently expresses more than it should. How to be an alien? One should not be an alien at all.

There are certain rules, however, which have to be followed if you want to make yourself as acceptable and civilized as you possibly can.

Study these rules, and imitate the English. There can be only one result: if you don't succeed in imitating them, you become ridiculous; if you do, you become even more ridiculous.

A WARNING TO BEGINNERS

In England,* everything is the other way around.

On Sundays on the Continent, even the poorest person puts on his best suit, tries to look respectable, and at the same time the life of the country becomes gay and cheerful; in England, even the richest peer or motor manufacturer dresses in some peculiar rags, does not shave, and the country becomes dull and dreary. On the Continent, there is one topic which should be avoided—the weather; in England, if you do not repeat the phrase "Lovely day, isn't it?" at least two hundred times a day, you are considered a bit dull. On the Continent, Sunday papers appear on Monday; in England—a country of exotic oddities—they appear on Sunday. On the Continent, people use a fork as though a fork were a shovel; in England, they turn it upside down and push everything—including peas—on top of it.

On a Continental bus approaching a request stop, the conductor rings the bell if he wants his bus to go on without stopping; in England, you ring the bell if you want the bus to stop. On the Continent, stray cats are judged individually on their merit—some are loved, some are only respected; in England, they are universally worshiped, as in ancient Egypt. On the Continent, people have good food; in England, people have good table manners.

On the Continent, public orators try to learn to speak fluently

* When people say England, they sometimes mean Great Britain, sometimes the United Kingdom, sometimes the British Isles—but never England.

and smoothly; in England, they take a special course in Oxonian stuttering. On the Continent, learned persons love to quote Aristotle, Horace, Montaigne and show off their knowledge; in England, only uneducated people show off their knowledge; nobody quotes Latin and Greek authors in the course of a conversation unless he has never read them.

On the Continent, almost every nation, whether little or great, has openly declared at one time or another that it is superior to all other nations; the English fight heroic wars to combat these dangerous ideas without ever mentioning which is *really* the superior race in the world. Continental people are sensitive and touchy; the English take everything with an exquisite sense of humor; they are only offended if you tell them that they have no sense of humor. On the Continent, the population consists of a small percentage of criminals, a small percentage of honest people, and the rest are a vague transition between the two; in England, you find a small percentage of criminals, and the rest are honest people. On the other hand, people on the Continent either tell you the truth or lie; in England, they hardly ever lie, but they would not dream of telling you the truth.

Many Continentals think life is a game; the English think cricket is a game.

INTRODUCTION

This is a chapter on how to introduce people to one another.

The aim of introduction is to conceal a person's identity. It is very important that you should not pronounce anybody's name in a way that the other party may be able to catch it. Generally speaking, your pronunciation is a sound guarantee of that. On the other hand, if you are introduced to someone, there are two important rules to follow.

1. If he stretches out his hand to shake yours, you must not accept it. Smile vaguely, and, as soon as he gives up the hope of

Sabbath morn

shaking you by the hand, you stretch out your own hand and try to catch *his* in vain. This game is repeated until the greater part of the afternoon or evening has elapsed. It is extremely likely that this will be the most amusing part of the afternoon or evening anyway.

2. Once the introduction has been made, you have to inquire after the health of your new acquaintance.

Try the thing in your own language. Introduce the persons, let us say, in French and murmur their names. Should they shake hands and ask:

"Comment allez-vous?"

"Comment allez-vous?"—it will be a capital joke, remembered to their last days.

Do not forget, however, that your new friend who makes this touchingly kind inquiry after your state of health does not care in the least whether you are well and kicking or dying of delirium tremens. A dialogue like this:

He: "How d'you do?"

You: "General state of health fairly satisfactory. Slight insomnia and a rather bad corn on left foot. Blood pressure low, digestion slow but normal."

Well, such a dialogue would be slightly out of place.

In the next phase, you must not say, "Pleased to meet you." This is one of the very few lies you must never utter because, for some unknown reason, it is considered vulgar. You must not say, "Pleased to meet you," even if you are definitely disgusted with the man.

A few general remarks:

1. Do not click your heels, do not bow, leave off gymnastic and choreographic exercises altogether for the moment.

2. Do not call foreign lawyers, teachers, dentists, commercial travelers, and estate agents "doctor." Everybody knows that the little word "doctor" only means that they are Central Europeans. This is painful enough in itself; you do not need to remind people of it all the time.

Which hand will you have?

THE WEATHER

This is the most important topic in the land. Do not be misled by memories of your youth, when, on the Continent, wanting to describe someone as exceptionally dull, you remarked: "He is the type who would discuss the weather with you." In England, this is an ever-interesting, even thrilling topic, and you must be good at discussing the weather.

EXAMPLES FOR CONVERSATION

For good weather

"Lovely day, isn't it?"
"Isn't it *beau*tiful?"
"The sun. . . ."
"Isn't it gorgeous?"
"Wonderful, isn't it?"
"It's so nice and hot. . . ."
"Personally, I think it's so nice when it's hot—isn't it?"
"I adore it—don't you?"

For bad weather

"Nasty day, isn't it?"
"Isn't it dreadful?"
"The rain . . . I hate rain. . . ."
"I don't like it at all. Do you?"
"Fancy such a day in July. Rain in the morning; then a bit of sunshine; and then rain, rain, rain, all day long."
"I remember exactly the same July day in 1936."
"Yes, I remember too."
"Or was it in 1928?"
"Yes, it was."
"Or in 1939?"
"Yes, that's right."

Now observe the last few sentences of this conversation. A very important rule emerges from it. You must never contradict anybody when discussing the weather. Should it hail and snow, should hurricanes uproot the trees from the sides of the road,

"Good afternoon!"

and should someone remark to you: "Nice day, isn't it?"—answer without hesitation: "Isn't it lovely?"

Learn the above conversation by heart. If you are a bit slow in picking things up, learn at least one conversation; it would do wonderfully for any occasion.

If you do not say anything else for the rest of your life, just repeat this conversation; you still have a fair chance of passing as a remarkably witty man of sharp intellect, keen observation, and extremely pleasant manners.

•

English society is a class society, strictly organized almost on corporative lines. If you doubt this, listen to the weather forecasts. There is always a different weather forecast for farmers. You often hear statements like this on the radio:

"Tomorrow it will be cold, cloudy, and foggy; long periods of rain will be interrupted by short periods of showers."

And then:

"Weather forecast for farmers. It will be fair and warm, many hours of sunshine."

You must not forget that the farmers do grand work of national importance and deserve better weather.

•

It has happened on innumerable occasions that nice, warm weather had been forecast and rain and snow fell all day long, or vice versa. Some people jump rashly to the conclusion that something must be wrong with the weather forecasts. They are mistaken and should be more careful with their allegations.

I have read an article in one of the Sunday papers, and now I can tell you what the situation really is. All troubles are caused by anticyclones. (I don't quite know what anticyclones are, but this is not important; I hate cyclones and am very anticyclone myself.) The two naughtiest anticyclones are the Azores and the Polar anticyclones.

The British meteorologists forecast the *right* weather—as it really *should* be—and then these impertinent little anticyclones interfere and mess up everything.

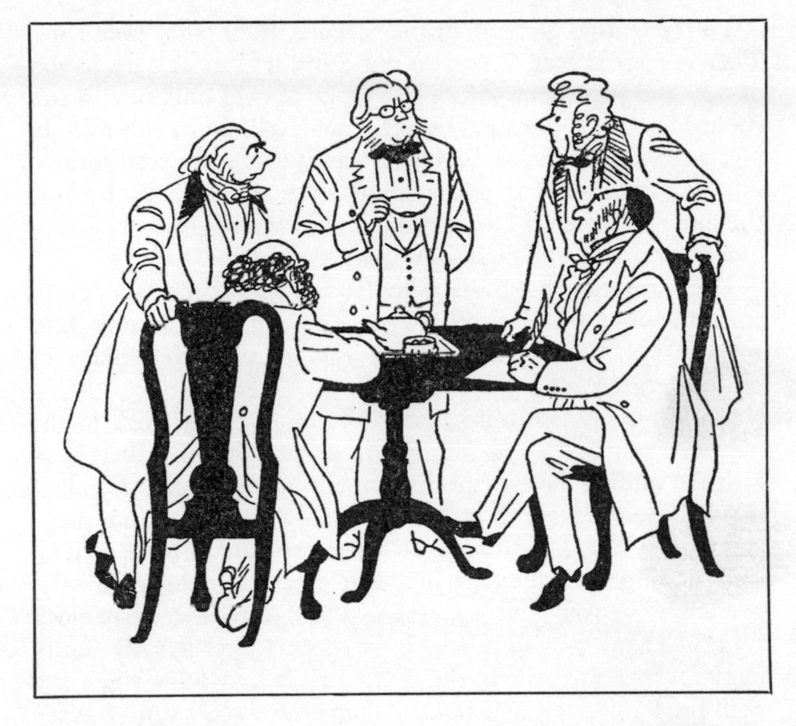

The cup that cheers

That again proves that, if the British kept to themselves and did not mix with foreign things like Polar and Azores anti-cyclones, they would be much better off.

TEA

The trouble with tea is that originally it was quite a good drink.

So a group of the most eminent British scientists put their heads together and made complicated biological experiments to find a way of spoiling it.

To the eternal glory of British science, their labor bore fruit. They suggested that, if you do not drink it clear or with lemon or rum and sugar, but pour a few drops of cold milk into it and no sugar at all, the desired object is achieved. Once this refreshing, aromatic, Oriental beverage was successfully transformed into colorless and tasteless gargling-water, it suddenly became the national drink of Great Britain and Ireland—still retaining, indeed usurping, the high-sounding title of tea.

There are some occasions when you must not refuse a cup of tea; otherwise you are judged an exotic and barbarous bird without any hope of ever being able to take your place in civilized society.

If you are invited to an English home, at five o'clock in the morning you get a cup of tea. It is brought in either by a heartily smiling hostess or by an almost malevolently silent maid. When you are disturbed in your sweetest morning sleep, you must not say: "Madame [or Mabel], I think you are a cruel, spiteful, and malignant person who deserves to be shot." On the contrary, you have to declare with your best five-o'clock smile: "Thank you so much. I do adore a cup of early morning tea, especially early in the morning." If they leave you alone with the liquid, you may pour it down the wash basin.

Then you have tea for breakfast; then you have tea at eleven o'clock in the morning; then after lunch; then you have tea for tea; then after supper; and again at eleven o'clock at night.

You must not refuse any additional cups of tea under the following circumstances: if it is hot; if it is cold; if you are tired; if anybody thinks that you might be tired; if you are nervous; if you are gay; before you go out; if you are out; if you have just returned home; if you feel like it; if you do not feel like it; if you have had no tea for some time; if you have just had a cup.

You definitely must not follow my example. I go to sleep at five o'clock in the morning; I have coffee for breakfast; I drink innumerable cups of black coffee during the day; I have the most unorthodox and exotic teas even at tea time.

The other day, for instance—I just mention this as a terrifying example to show you how low some people can sink—I wanted a cup of coffee and a piece of cheese for tea. It was one of those exceptionally hot days, and my wife (once a good Englishwoman, now led completely and hopelessly astray by my wicked foreign influence) made some cold coffee and put it in the refrigerator, where it froze and became one solid block. On the other hand, she left the cheese on the kitchen table, where it melted. So I had a piece of coffee and a glass of cheese.

SEX

Continental people have sex life; the English have hot-water bottles.

HOW NOT TO BE CLEVER

"You foreigners are so clever," said a lady to me some years ago. First, thinking of the great number of foreign idiots and halfwits I had had the honor of meeting, I considered this remark exaggerated but complimentary.

Since then I have learned that it was far from it. These few words expressed the lady's contempt and slight disgust for foreigners.

If you look up the word "clever" in any English dictionary, you will find that the dictionaries are out of date and mislead you on this point. According to one dictionary, for instance, the word means quick and neat in movement . . . skilful, talented, ingenious. Another gives these meanings: dexterous, skillful, ingenious, quick- or ready-witted, intelligent. All nice adjectives, expressing valuable and estimable characteristics. A modern Englishman, however, uses the word "clever" in the sense: shrewd, sly, furtive, surreptitious, treacherous, sneaking, crafty, un-English, un-Scottish, un-Welsh.

In England, it is bad manners to be clever, to assert something confidently. It may be your personal view that two and two make four, but you must not state it in a self-assured way, because it is a democratic country, and others may be of a different opinion.

A Continental gentleman seeing a nice panorama may remark:

> This view rather reminds me of Utrecht, where the peace treaty concluding the War of Spanish Succession was signed on April 11, 1713. The river there, however, recalls the Guadalquivir, which rises in the Sierra de Cazorla, flows southwest to the Atlantic Ocean, and is 650 kilometers long. Oh, rivers. . . . What did Pascal say about them? "Les rivières sont les chemins qui marchent. . . ."

This pompous, showing-off way of speaking is not permissible in England. The Englishman is modest and simple. He uses but few words and expresses so much—but so much—with them. An Englishman looking at the same view would remain silent for two or three hours and think about how to put his profound feelings into words. Then he would remark: "It's pretty, isn't it?"

An English professor of mathematics would say to his maid adding up the shopping list: "I'm no good at arithmetic, I'm afraid. Please correct me, Jane, if I am wrong, but I believe that the square root of 97,344 is 312."

And about knowledge. An English girl, of course, would be able to learn just a little more about, let us say, geography. But it is just not "chic" to know whether Budapest is the capital of Rumania, Hungary, or Bulgaria. And, if she happens to know that Budapest *is* the capital of Rumania, she should at least be perplexed if Bucharest is mentioned suddenly.

It is so much nicer to ask, when someone speaks of Barbados, Banska Bystrica, or Fiji:

"Oh, those little islands. . . . Are they British?"

(They often are, even today.)

"*Dr. Hoffmeyer is absolutely* brilliant"

2

√ BRITAIN
FRANCE
ITALY
GERMANY
SWITZERLAND
ISRAEL
JAPAN

PROUST AND CÔTE DE VEAU

In Hungary, I was taught that France was a Great Power; in England, I was told that France was a great joke. When I was a small child, Hungary was going through one of her periodic collapses, and this time—after World War I—France was the distant and mighty military power who—as it seemed to us—was the cause of it all. Rumania and the new states of Czechoslovakia and Yugoslavia became the masters of our part of Europe because France was their friend and ally; Hungary, on the other hand, was humiliated and deprived of territory and population because France frowned on her. These first childish memories left an indelible impression on my mind, and I was greatly surprised to find in England—in 1938—that Englishmen were always referring to France with a twinkle in their eyes and that elderly guardians of morality always blushed at the mention of

Paris. France used to mean naked force to me; it meant naked breasts to them.

I have heard, of course, many other views on France. For Central Europeans, France, in addition to being the grim and gigantic military power—the reshaper of the map of Europe and the power that occupied the Ruhr—was also the Mecca of Western culture, the gay land of an eternal *vie de bohème* and, at the same time, the country of Anatole France and Proust, Rodin, and Renoir. Others declared angrily that France was a political brothel, and again others retorted that they did not know what was political about it.

France's profile, as seen from the East, differed considerably, then, from the Western view. By now I have seen many other snapshots taken from various angles and observation points. For postwar Germany, France was the great example: "How to lose a war and win it," the Germans murmured with surprise and admiration and went on to improve on the French methods. For many Americans, France is a nuisance today, and hardly more than a nuisance, because the French still think of themselves as Frenchmen instead of as cogs in the huge defense system against Communism. For many despairing yet amused Europeans, France is the country of a wild, Walpurgis-nightish game of musical chairs, played, until recently, by incoming and outgoing prime ministers.

I have tried to rid myself of stupid prejudices, but, of course, I have not been able to do so. To love a nation is as much of a prejudice as to hate one; if you love one, you are almost certain to hate another. All the same, I love the French. They are all *petits choux*; they are all Little Cabbages. If I could choose what to be, I think, I should like to be a Frenchman. A naturalized Frenchman, living in England.

LATIN CLARITY

If you want to become a proper Frenchman or at least understand the French, you must comprehend Latin Clarity. Latin

Clarity is the name of a special French kind of muddle. Its distinguishing features are that it is neither Latin nor clear. The foundation of Latin Clarity is the childish but unshakable belief that (1) things are what they look, (2) they look what they are, and that (3) a definition defines anything.

All nations are very proud of the special kind of muddle they practice and believe in. The ultimate argument people love to use in a certain kind of dispute is to declare—with misty eyes, staring into space—that a specific type of reasoning is much too English, French, German, much too Bulgarian, or much too Persian for you to understand. In my native country, it was officially maintained between the two wars that to compel people to cast their vote openly in parliamentary elections—under the keen and interested eye of the *gendarme* and the tax inspector—was real democracy—in fact, real democracy with improvements. The argument was convincing, but, I fear, much too Hungarian for you to grasp.

The English find muddle their natural element. They dislike and distrust order. If they succeed in mellowing chaos into normal and acceptable disorder, they call it order. They hate reasoning and possess the instinctive adroitness to reduce any problem to its illogical conclusions. The English obey a constitution which does not exist. They administer almost ideal justice based on what is by far the worst and most archaic legal system in the civilized world. They are strongly against alcoholism, so they close their pubs at certain times when no one wants to drink in any case. The Anglican Church regards gambling as one of the most odious vices and consequently fights for the right to be allowed to organize lotteries, football pools, and so on. The English abhor commercial radio, but allow commercial television. They combine complete freedom of expression with a strict censorship and habeas corpus with the law that a person may be arrested for an *intention;* and some good socialists crown their career of a lifelong struggle against inequality by becoming Peers of the Realm. The unassailable strength of English common sense is the conviction that reasoning must not be carried too far; indeed, reasoning is only permitted during proper hours.

The French and the Germans, on the other hand, have principles, and all manner of follies and absurdities logically follow from these admirable principles. Surprisingly enough, the Germans, too, possess a small amount of Latin Clarity. The democratic constitution of Weimar contained—as do all proper democratic constitutions—the seeds of its own destruction, and it was, in fact, destroyed. The postwar Germans tried to find stronger and better safeguards, while the Russians tried quite a different approach to the same problem. They have the only constitution which is even more democratic and more liberal than the late Weimar constitution was. I defy anyone to read through the Soviet constitution without being moved to tears. At the same time, it is a capital offense in Russia to claim one's constitutional rights. This is Slav Clarity.

In England, if you—being a man—invite a young lady to visit your apartment, you may genuinely have several prospects in mind; in France, you may only have one. In England, if you go into a restaurant, you may have a series of reasons for so doing, ranging from a desire to dance to a desire to save on income tax; in France, you presumably want to eat. In England, you put a napkin across your lap, and in this way you may make the napkin dirty without keeping yourself clean; in France, you may tuck the napkin into your collar and make yourself utterly ridiculous by using the napkin as though it were a napkin. In England, the horn of your car is used in the same way as an Englishman's voice—for an occasional friendly or unfriendly grunt. In France, the horn is built into the driver's seat, and you sit on it. If you want to give a signal for one reason or another, you lift yourself up for a moment and make yourself conspicuous by not honking for a second or two. But, when it was discovered that honking is morally wrong, it was absolutely prohibited, abolished, almost forgotten. The French draw a clear distinction between leisure and work: they either work or they don't. In England, work is a leisurely kind of activity between cups of tea. The English, in fact, have such a wonderful rest during working hours that, as soon as they get home, they indulge in heavy physical labor such as digging the garden, painting a room, or playing golf. A Frenchman smiles if he is pleased and shouts if he is angry; an Englishman is silent when pleased and even more silent when angry.

The French know all the laws of this world and expect things and events to follow them with logic. The trouble with the universe is that it possesses much less Latin Clarity than the French, and always the illogical, the unexpected, the impossible—sometimes even the improbable—happens. But this is the fault of the universe and not of the French.

HOW TO BE DECADENT

You simply *must* become decadent if you want to make any progress at all in becoming French. For years and years, we have heard about French decadence. Take the case of the falling birth rate, for example. Some people say that the French cannot think of an effective way of raising the falling birth rate; others are of the opinion that they cannot think of anything else.

It is not difficult to become decadent. In fact, it is child's play. I am very decadent myself, but I must admit that decadence comes easier to a Central European than to Englishmen. English people need much practice if they are to succeed.

Nevertheless, I personally shall never make a really first-class decadent because I love people. I love everybody—or almost everybody. All those in dire need of love should just flock to my bosom. I am also a born optimist and an idealist in a mild and unrapturous way, and all this will not do for a true prodigy of decadence. A nondecadent—a person of vigor, bounding energy, stamina, and bloom—surveys the global landscape and rubs his hands with joy. He looks sturdily in the future, exclaims: "Splendid!" and radiates optimism. Or, better still, does not even take the trouble to look about him or into the future. He just reads a thriller or the comics or goes to films featuring nondecadent cowboys.

In France, you may make fun of anything you wish. The French may not laugh, but they will shrug their shoulders. In Germany, you may joke about sex, but not about the Fatherland. In England, where the very word "Fatherland" is a joke, sex jokes are not appreciated or, in many cases, even understood. Sex in France has always a farcical, in England an obscene, undertone. In America, you are not permitted to make jokes—I mean jokes that really sting—about the American destiny, about their glorious Constitution, their so-called way of life, and their general wisdom and nobility of heart. The Germans are afraid of their patriotism, the English of sex life, and the Americans of themselves. The French are in many ways worse off than any of the others; but they are not afraid. And not to be afraid is extremely decadent.

The Germans regard the French as decadent because France was brought to her knees during the war—although in the end she gained the upper hand. The Americans regard the French as decadent because they still prefer red wine to brown Coca Cola and colonialism in Africa to colonialism in Europe.

The basic rules for being decadent are these:

(1) Do not get overexcited if you see something known to you for 150 years dressed up as novelty. Say: "Déja vu." Say it in French. To say it in any other language is not decadent.

(2) Cherish the style—and never mind the substance.

(3) Forget words such as black and white, good and evil, generous and cruel. Learn expressions such as these: "ambivalent," "interdependent," "so-so," and "hm. . . ." Write on paper and not on banners. Express yourself in plain words not in plain slogans. Learn to doubt motives but appreciate and acknowledge results.

(4) Sit down and relax. It is true that we live in historic,

Decadence

critical, momentous, and epoch-making times, but we have done this for so long that there is nothing thrilling about it any more. One gets used to making epochs. Learn the beauty of uselessness, the pleasure of wasting time. Learn how to temper suffering with epigrams. Do not believe that rushing about noisily and frantically is the equivalent of doing something worthwhile.

•

To be decadent means more or less to be European. There is nothing to be proud of in being European—but what can we do? What can we possibly be between Asia and America? So let us decay in our chosen manner and in our own distinguished company. We respect other peoples' way of life: let them respect our way of decay. It's fun. I, for one, enjoy it.

THE NATIONAL PASSION

The French have many national habits, but their national passion is saving. Other peoples save, too, but none like the French. They save as the Spaniards watch bullfights; as the Sicilians bask in the sunshine; as the Finns bathe in their saunas; as the Norwegians retreat to lonely mountain huts; as the English queue up; and as the Americans chew gum.

In prewar Hungary, people used to live far above their station and sigh longingly: "I wish I could afford to live in the style in which I am actually living." But, quite to the contrary, the dream of the average Frenchman is to become a millionaire and then starve. They want to be able to afford all the things they never dream of doing. Not to be able to travel or build a nice and comfortable house is frustrating. But to be able to afford it and yet save the money instead—this seems the summit of their ambition and the climax of earthly pleasure. There are many lovely, romantic, and expensive things Frenchmen never do, so saving is not only a thrilling and exciting pastime but also one full of variety. There are so many wonderful things to miss, if only you use your imagination and are able to discriminate.

French peasants are reputed to keep their money in the mattress or in socks. They do not trust the banks. (My personal dream is that an embezzler in my bank will one day elope with

Nation of savers

my overdraft.) Not only peasants save in France, and the sock—real and symbolic—figures large in French life. It is a mentality that cuts deep and—just to mention one example—the building of the Maginot Line was, in fact, an attempt to hide the whole country in a gigantic, historic sock.

France used to be one of the wealthiest countries in the world, and still is a land of vast riches. This statement may sound surprising to people who have judged France by the dreariness and squalor of her villages—in other words, people who were taken in by the French mania for saving and inverted showing-off.

•

The French spend, or try to spend, their lives in saving small fortunes. A Frenchman looks forward to retirement as the final aim of his working life. He works in order to be able to stop working. He looks forward to feeble old age with gusto. To eat without teeth is one of the ultimate delights of living. And, since even a Frenchman is not completely lacking in small personal vanities, he dreams of a smart funeral. He works hard throughout a lifetime to be able to die above his station.

•

Even economists do not quite understand these mysterious and puzzling phenomena. How is it possible, they ask themselves, that once upon a time all Frenchmen were able to save? On what? And, if that was so, why is it not so any more? These economists have invented many theories, but have never been able to hit the nail on the head. So I'd better give them the explanation.

All male and foreign visitors to France know that there is a certain natural and much too frequently recurring function of the human body which costs much money in France. Wherever we go on a certain errand, we see corpulent ladies sitting next to white plates, and these plates gape at us like the monstrous Cyclopean eye of our own consciences. Dutifully and meekly, we spend three pennies whenever we go to spend one, whether in splendid cafés or dirty, unattended contraptions (obviously built in the spirit of the slogan that "Frenchmen have nothing to hide"), whether in Paris or in the provinces, in palaces or in huts. Many a prosperous foreigner has gone to the dogs by visiting these places without sobriety and moderation.

What has all this to do with the French economy? A great deal. Since this obligation only hangs over the head—if this be the right metaphor—of foreigners, all Frenchmen could, and did, save large sums by being exempt from this heavy toll. Just having a place of your own in France means a net, annual saving of about $300 per person.

THE ART OF SITTING IN CAFÉS

You sit in a café and watch people walking up and down in front of it; then you walk up and down in front of the café and give other people a chance to watch you. As a member of that strolling or surging crowd, you have become one of the sights of Paris; you have become a rival of the Eiffel Tower.

Why do they have cafés in France? Or, why do they not have cafés—worthy of the name—in Britain? What the English call a café is a purely utilitarian establishment; you go in for a cup of coffee or tea or a light snack, and, as soon as you have swallowed it, you hurry out. In a French café, you are both a sightseer and an object of sightseeing. You have your appointments there; you meet your friends in the cafés instead of meeting them in your office, drawing-room, or club; you sit there dreaming or watching life around you; you spend an odd hour or two—or an odd five hours, if it suits you. To be able to do all this, you have to consume a coffee, a piece of cake, a brandy, or a liqueur. The meal is simply an excuse—a ticket. An edible ticket, or a ticket containing a high percentage of alcohol, but a ticket all the same.

These differing attitudes to cafés reflect differing attitudes to life. A nation or society expresses its character as clearly in the way it sits in its cafés as in its attitude toward its armed forces, its administration of justice, its literature, its jokes, or its manner of driving. The Englishman's outlook is practical. He has, if not a mission, at least a more-or-less definite purpose in the café, as he has in life. Nothing too important, but nevertheless closely defined. Not that he has a sense of mission in the German sense of the word, but, while on this globe, he might as well pass his time doing something useful or something useless but innocent and pleasant. He may become an accomplished golfer; he may learn Latin; he may grow tomatoes in a glass house; he may dedicate his life to finding out absolutely everything about Sherlock Holmes and Dr. Watson. And he may drop into a café for a cup of tea with milk but without sugar. The Frenchman, on the other hand, has no special purpose on this earth or in the café. But, once there, he is trying to make the best of it. If it is not quite clear what our aim is in life, it is a shade clearer what life's aim is with us. Similarly, the Frenchman may wish to do many things in the café; but the café expects only one thing from him—to order something and pay for it. The Frenchman performs his duty. Not perfunctorily, not grudgingly—indeed, he tries to make it as pleasant for himself as he can. Yet, what ought to be the purpose of his visit, the café's *raison d'être*, remains only a side issue for him.

For the German, life is a mission of major importance. Life is finite; man is mortal. The only way the German can bear the idea of mortality is by trying to make himself immortal—as an individual or as a nation, by peace or by war, by chasing an ideal or by chasing foreign armies. For the Englishman, life is an errand of minor importance. It is not a cataclysm; it is a cocktail party. He arrives, has a mildly pleasant time, and does not overstay his welcome. There is nothing tragic in departure; the invitation clearly said: 6–8. He plays the game. To live longer than he is supposed to is poor form; it simply isn't cricket. Have you had your tea? Your chair is needed, others are waiting. For the Frenchman, life is an opportunity. He does not go to the café to have a Pernod, but, once there, he has one. It is far from certain that he lives in order to flirt with women; but it is quite certain that, if he wants to flirt, he has to be alive.

Kant tried to explain *why* we live; Rousseau how we should live; Berkeley wasn't quite sure whether we are alive at all. Different cafés, different patrons.

•

The cafés, like life itself, have their deep mysteries. For me, the mystery men of the French café are the Arabs, and, first of all, the Arab carpet-dealers. Who buys carpets in cafés?—I often ask myself wistfully. And how is it done? Quite casually? You go into the café for an ice cream. The carpet-dealer appears, calling out: "Fine Arab carpets, fine Arab carpets," rather as our news-vendors shout: "Evening paper!" You look at him and say to yourself: "Oh, carpets . . . well, I might as well buy a carpet. Come to think of it, I haven't bought a carpet for weeks." And you buy one—nine by twelve feet—and put it under your arm and dash away to your next appointment with your bank manager, your dentist, or your girl friend. Is this how it's done? Or do you just catch sight of the carpet-dealers and exclaim: "Good heavens! Now I remember: I haven't a carpet on me." (Searching all your pockets:) "I am forgetful! . . . . I must have left all my carpets at home. How annoying." And you buy one in a hurry just so as not to be without a carpet for the day.

Another group of mysterious Arabs gives you monkey nuts. They do not sell monkey nuts—they distribute them free of charge. They walk up to your table, lay one nut down, and depart. As you eat the nut, you think: "Who says there isn't real charity, goodness, unselfishness, and nobility of heart left in the world?"

Maybe the Arab nut-distributors belong to a small but distinguished religious sect which commands its followers: "Go ye forth and distribute monkey nuts unto people in Paris cafés." Or maybe they are employed by a fabulously rich Arab oil magnate who is burdened by the memory of a horrible crime which he seeks to expiate by distributing nuts free of charge to the rich and undeserving.

I do not know. The Nut-Giver remains an unfathomable mystery to me. My own explanation is that the Nut-Givers are in league with the carpet-dealers. Whenever I received my piece of nut, I was so overwhelmed by this manifestation of human kindness and brotherly love that I always—absolutely without fail—bought a carpet from the next dealer who turned up.

But this explanation is cynical and quite unworthy of me. Life swarms with exciting mysteries. One of them is: "What is our aim on this earth?" Another: "Why do Arabs distribute free nuts in the coffee houses of a Great and Sinful Western City?"

•

A final word on the Art of Sitting in Cafés. The French have invented a wonderful way of making coffee—the system of the *café filtre*. Or was it the Belgians who originally thought of the idea? Whoever the inventors were, beware of the *café filtre*. I do not mind that the coffee it produces is not good; I do not mind that the filter is always blocked so that the coffee does not drip through or that, when it does, it drips so slowly that the coffee is cold by the time it is through. I could forgive the *filtre* all these weaknesses—after all, it is only human. But I do not forgive it for its truly nasty, wicked, and spiteful character. Whenever I wish to prompt it to a quicker and more efficient performance of its duty by removing the lid and pushing the little nickel bar down with my finger, it suddenly starts behaving like a magic fountain and squirts a graceful jet of boiling hot coffee into my eye. Well, I do not mind honest criticism; but I do object to being spat at by a defaulting gadget.

A MAN OF MYSTERY

Paris has always been an irresistible magnet for eccentric and quixotic people. In Paris I met the most surprising *émigré* in the world. One morning I had apéritifs with two friends; one is the editor of a literary and political magazine, and the other, a historian. Both are Swiss, and their mother tongue is German.

The editor told us that he knew of a wonderful Indonesian

Actually bought a carpet

restaurant nearby which he would like to try. Our faces darkened because we knew that he was fond of reckless and foolish adventures. I asked him how, if he had never been there, he knew that the restaurant was wonderful. The historian—a man of very quiet disposition—remarked that in Paris he had found French restaurants quite satisfactory and that he would prefer to stick to them. But we were both fully aware that we were fighting a losing battle.

The editor declared that he did not know exactly where the Indonesian restaurant was, but it was not far from the Hôtel de Ville and, if we would just drive up and down all the streets in that neighborhood, combing the district with conscientious care, we were bound to find it. We set out on our errand—the historian and I, with a deep sigh; the editor with exuberant joy. We found the place in five minutes.

The restaurant consisted of two rooms. There were no guests in the first. Three Indonesian girls—obviously employees of the establishment—were having lunch at a corner table and at the same time lending some local color to the place. We proceeded to the inner room, where we found a gentleman standing behind the bar. He was a tall, muscular man with fair hair. His un-Indonesian appearance was conspicuous even to the most superficial observer.

We greeted him and ordered some drinks in French. The *patron*'s French was fluent, but he had a foreign accent which I could not place. We three were conversing in English, and, after a few minutes, the *patron* joined in the conversation. In English his accent was easily recognizable; it was obviously German. A short while afterward the editor and the historian began to speak German, and the *patron* joined in this conversation, too. My German is not what it should be, but, as I listened, I felt certain that the man was now talking in his mother tongue. And, after some further listening, I was almost sure he was talking in a Sudeten-German accent—which is very characteristic and easily recognizable.

The *patron* turned to me and asked:

"Are you an Englishman?"

Since I wanted to avoid lengthy explanations, I replied briefly:

"I am."

But he was not satisfied and went on inquiring:

"From which town, if I may ask?"

"From Budapest," I answered casually.

He seemed to be surprised.

"You are an Englishman from Budapest?"

"Yes," I nodded modestly.

"But how is that?" he went on pressing me like a man who instinctively feels that he has hold of a good, almost decisive, point in an argument. "How can you be an Englishman from Budapest?"

"Why not?" I replied, "if you can be an Indonesian from Karlsbad?"

You could have knocked him down with a feather. He really did come from Karlsbad. I guessed right by mistake, so to speak, because I thought Karlsbad is a Sudeten town, which it is not; but it was the only town I could remember in that part of the world.

When we settled down to have our lunch, I asked him:

"Now we know the basic truth about each other," I said. "But I don't think I know enough about you yet. If I am not being too inquisitive, please tell me. How—just how—does a Sudeten-German refugee from Karlsbad become an Indonesian restaurateur in Paris?"

He looked at me with big, sad eyes. Then he shrugged his shoulders and made a gesture, turning both palms outward:

"Man hat Ideen . . .," he replied. "One has a little idea here and there. . . ."

•

I was deeply impressed. What he said was, in fact, the solution of a great deal of seemingly unfathomable human mystery one encounters in life. One has a little idea here and there, that's all.

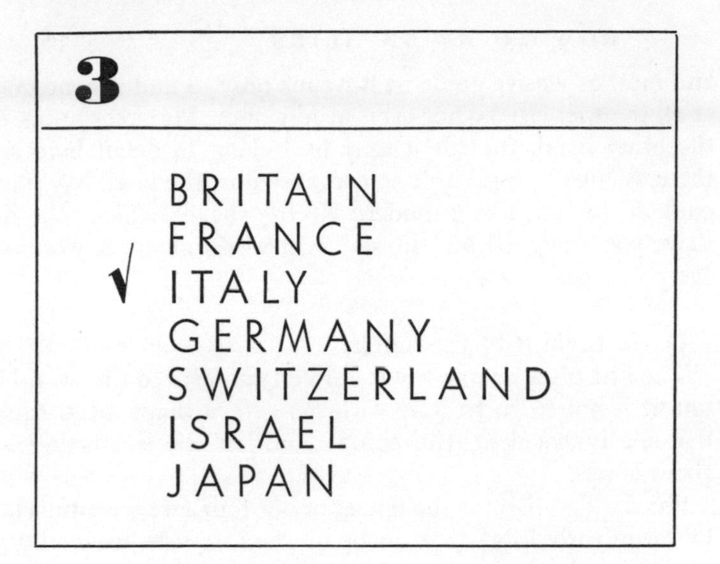

HOTELS

Do you want to be a tourist or a native in Italy? It is easier to be a tourist, cheaper to be a native.

I shall give my advice first to tourists and turn to the natives afterward. Having been—as I have said—so deeply impressed by travel guides, I have here compiled, in the following few pages, one of my own. My travel guide is an immense improvement on all its predecessors, and it ought to have a special appeal to our American cousins because of its brevity and conciseness. When visiting a cathedral with my guidebook in hand you need not bother to find out whether you are in Pisa, Naples, or Venice. My description applies equally to all the cathedrals in Italy. The same goes for the towns. Maps—like life in general—have become much too specialized in modern times; it is a tremendous drawback of the otherwise excellent maps of, say, Perugia that they are practically useless in Modena. Or you may buy the best and most expensive guide to Ravenna only to find it is no good at all in other cities—not even nearby ones. My description, on the other hand, though it may be lacking in detail here and there, is equally applicable to every town in the land. My travel guide is, in fact, like a modern electric shaver, which may not shave you very well but, insofar as it works at all, it works on every voltage.

•

Let us begin with the hotels.

The first piece of important advice I can give to the would-be tourist is not to go to Italy with my wife. I don't mean to say that she isn't a delightful companion, but she is a little fussy about hotels.

She decided right at the outset of our tour (we were traveling by car in early July) that, to be on the safe side, we would go only to hotels which were (1) recommended *both* by our guidebook and by the AAA book, (2) were not too expensive, (3) not too cheap, (4) were not in the noisy center of the town, but (5) not far away from the center.

Arriving then at, let us say, Florence, she would read out an address: Hotel X, Piazza della Republica. From there to Hotel Y, Piazza Santa Novella. Then: Hotel Z, Via della Scala, and so on and so on almost indefinitely. In the first dozen hotels, there would be no vacant rooms at all. In the thirteenth, she would refuse an attractive room because the porter had a saucy moustache and might turn out to be offensive. In the fourteenth, she would turn a room down because the ceiling was too high and she thought it might be difficult to heat such a room in February. In the fifteenth, there would be another room smack opposite ours, and "What if there is a baby in that room that would cry all night?" Whereupon she would produce the address of the sixteenth hotel, on the Lungarno Amerigo Vespucci. Then I would meekly remark that my early training had qualified me to become a lawyer in Budapest, not a taxi driver in Florence. She would not be amused, and off we would drive to the Lungarno Amerigo Vespucci.

If, at the end of an eight or ten hours' search we had landed in the dreariest hole in the lousiest and most expensive guest house in Tuscany, I was happy and content because I felt vindicated; but, whenever we did find a good room at a reasonable price (and we often did). I was very, very disconsolate.

•

Although you are not traveling with my wife, do no imagine that your position will be all that much easier.

Why are Italian hotels full all the time? Because of the engineers' conferences.

We could not get a room in Verona because—we were told—the engineers were having a conference in the town. We could not get a room in Padua because the same engineers—or perhaps other engineers—were having a conference there, too. A few weeks later, I could not get a room in Trieste (I was then by myself). "There is not a single room to be had in the whole town," a hotel porter told me. "The best thing you can do is to drive to Udine or Monfalcone and try there. Even there, you may find it difficult." He added in explanation: "You see, the engineers are having a conference in the town."

In no travel guide is this basic fact mentioned, that engineers are having a conference in all Italian towns all the time.

I saw many of these engineers; I could not help seeing them. We usually met at breakfast time. Every hotel restaurant was teeming between 8 and 9:30 A.M. with gay and lively engineers—ready for breakfast and eager to confer afterward. They all wore a red or blue label of some kind in their buttonholes. They brought curious objects out of enormous briefcases. The object—more often than not—consisted of a metal rod with a ring in the middle, in which there was a boxlike instrument which could be rotated round the rod. At the end of the rod there was something they could pull out and push in again. The object seemed rather dull and childish to the lay eye, but it was a source of endless delight, fascination, and awe to all engineers.

So what—I asked myself—if one cannot get a room in

Italian hotels? It is indeed a small price to pay for the happiness of the engineers.

•

Of course, you may always have a room reserved in advance; and, if you receive a confirmation from an Italian hotel stating that a room has, in fact, been reserved for you, that may mean many things. It does not even entirely exclude the possibility that a room has been reserved for you. But it would be almost enchanting naïveté to count on it.

In Rome, for example, they accept 20 per cent more reservations than the number of people they can accommodate. People who have rooms reserved often do not turn up; but then, again, they often do, and that's just too bad for them. In the season, hundreds of people are turned away from hotels in Rome—people who booked and were accepted. Many people are driven to the conclusion that it is simpler to be turned away from hotels without previous reservation.

In any Italian city after five or six in the afternoon, you may see people in cars—foreign and provincial cars—slowly and sadly cruising the town. The car is overloaded with luggage; the husband is driving; his wife is anxiously scrutinizing a clumsily folded map and directing her husband—usually in the wrong direction. This overcrowding of hotels and consequent desperate search for rooms, I was told, is extremely beneficial economically:

(1) the cruising motorists use up gasoline, thus helping the oil companies;

(2) they frequently stop for refreshments, thus helping the food industry;

(3) they ensure that all the hotels are full all the time, and that is why hotel-keepers resist all attempts to build more hotels.

So what—I asked myself again—if one cannot get a room in any hotel in Italy? Is it not indeed a small price to pay for the happiness of oil companies, caterers, and hotel-keepers?

•

"Conferenza dei Ingenieri"

Yet, however often one is told that it is impossible to get a room in an Italian hotel since all the hotels are always full, there seems to be a flaw in this reasoning. Hotels must be full of people who actually did succeed in getting rooms. Indeed, I should go as far as to say that, the fuller the hotels are, the more people managed to get in.

•

Finally, just one more word. Hotel bills are scrupulously honest all over Italy. If here and there in some of the smaller places they happen to add the date to the bill, it is an error, committed in perfectly good faith. The only case which puzzled me occurred in Naples. I wondered whether they were justified in adding 230 lire for heating to my bill in the midst of a July heat wave.

THE CATHEDRAL

Before entering the Cathedral, take a good look at the impressive and wonderful square itself. It is the third largest square in Italy and was planned by Michelangelo himself. Or, rather, by a group of his best pupils under Michelangelo's personal supervision. Or, anyway, someone just as good as Michelangelo or a trifle better. By all means have a good look at this magnificent square, but do not linger, spellbound by all that immortal beauty, because somebody will sell you a Parker 51 fountain pen before you can say Jack Robinson.

The cathedral of this ancient and beautiful city of . . . . .* is of particular interest. It is the third largest cathedral in Italy. It is a magnificent Gothic building (not pure Gothic, but pure enough for the vast majority of tourists). It was started in 1123 and consecrated in 1611, but was not completely finished until July 16, 1727. The Italians, in their outlandish way, like to refer to the Cathedral as *Il Duomo*. This is an ancient habit of theirs. It is, in fact, the third most ancient habit of the Italians.

Inside, there are 267 marble steps in the spiral stairway which

* Fill in the name of the city with pencil. Erase it afterward.

is the third highest spiral stairway in Italy. (If you take the elevator, it costs 200 lire extra.) You will probably be struck by the vast number of statues and busts in the Cathedral; there are 673 of them altogether. There are only two other cathedrals in the whole of Italy with more statues.

On the right-hand side, under the first arch of the main nave, you can see Ghirlandaio's world-famous picture, "The Last Judgment." Walk straight on, and on the same side you will find "The Wedding at Cana," by Fra Filippo Lippi. It is also worthwhile paying a visit to the Treasury (200 lire extra), where you can see a golden chalice given by Charlemagne to the pope and a silver chalice given by the pope to Charlemagne. There is also an ancient cloak which Philip II of Spain sent to the pope. Its counterpart—the cloak sent by the pope to Philip—can be seen in practically every cathedral in Spain.

The wonderful stained glass windows on the left are the great pride of the *Duomo*.* They were made by Leonardo da Vinci himself. Or by a pupil of Leonardo. Or someone else just as good as Leonardo or considerably better.

Before leaving the cathedral, you must go down the steps opposite the stone coffins of the three twelfth-century archbishops. There you can see the tomb of the Saint. More often than not, it is the tomb of St. George, who killed the dragon. The popularity of any one saint in Italy may be gauged by the number of cathedrals in which he (or she) is buried. At the moment, St. George holds a comfortable lead, with twenty-three tombs. St. Sebastian is second, with nineteen. There is a dead heat—if this be the right expression—for the third place between St. Augustine and St. Benedict (thirteen tombs each).

The tomb itself—in this cathedral—is behind a magnificent wrought-iron gate. It is, as a rule, littered with money—coins and notes just thrown over the gate. According to the popular belief, the Saint will perform a miracle in return for monetary sacrifice. Small miracles can be performed from 100 lire upward (fifty lire for soldiers and children under twelve). Really

* Italian for "cathedral."

miraculous miracles start at 1,000 lire per miracle (2,000 lire at the height of the tourist season).

THE TOWN

Leaving the Cathedral, cross the square and turn sharp left. You must not fail to make an intensive tour of the town, which is one of the most beautiful and ancient towns in Italy. It was built as an Etruscan village, but during Roman times it was inhabited mostly by Romans. After the downfall of Rome, it was occupied by the barbarians from the North, then by the barbarians from the East, and later by the barbarians from the North again. In the tenth and eleventh centuries, it was the battleground of feuding lords. In the twelfth century, it became an independent republic, and, to celebrate its independence, a large number of heretics were burned alive in the market square. The town was occupied by Napoleon, who put one of his brothers on the throne; later it was occupied by the Austrians, who were succeeded by the French, who were succeeded by the Austrians. The republic joined the Kingdom of Italy in 1860.

Many buildings which have survived centuries of strife and destruction are veritable masterpieces; many buildings which have not survived were also veritable masterpieces. In the third street on the right, you find the *Museo*,* containing one of the finest art collections in Italy. Coming out of the *Museo*, turn sharp right again and go down the beautiful Renaissance marble staircase; turn sharp left and come up again. In the Church of San Giovanni (one of the finest Renaissance churches in Italy), you can see Tintoretto's masterpiece, "Madonna with Four Saints." In the Church of San Giacomo, you can see Botticelli's masterpiece, "Two Saints with the Madonna." In the Church of San Bartolomeo, do not miss Tiepolo's huge canvas, "Madonna with Twenty-Three Saints." In the chapel of San

* Museum, really.

Monetary sacrifice

Marco, the focus of attention is Perugino's small painting, "Madonna with Just One Saint."

Admission to most of these churches is free except for the few hundred lire you are expected to give the priest at the main door. (Useless to try the side door, there is another priest there.)

(In Rome, in the Church of San Pietro in Vincoli—the home of Michelangelo's "Moses"—a priest stops you to inquire: why do you wish to go in? Should you say: to see "Moses," you are required to pay 200 lire, which sum, however, is not an entrance fee but a voluntary contribution on your part. If your intention is to pray, entrance is free. If you want to go in both to pray *and* to see "Moses," you pay half price.)

Proceeding toward the right, you reach the fortress built between 1254 and 1355. Now it is used as a museum.† Opposite is the Palazzo, ancient home of the Podestá, now used as a museum. The next building on the right is the old museum, now used as a palazzo.

Leaving the Palazzo, you enter the Old Town, which is extremely Medieval with a dash of Renaissance. In the Old Town, as well as in all the outlying districts, you can see a number of romantic people. Most of them are very hungry, which is also romantic. They are clad in picturesque rags, which in winter time become even more picturesque. Many of these people have a romantic smell.

Then you stop to think a little. Most of the riches and beauty of Italy have been handed down from ancient times. Not all, of course; Italian opera—to mention only one example—is a recent phenomenon. Yet, on the whole, apart from Italy's natural beauty, which is eternal, her man-made beauty consists either of Roman ruins or art treasures, the most recent of which are three hundred years old. No country can match Italy's wealth, and few countries can match Italy's poverty. The problem the Italians seem to have solved (at least until

† *Museo*, in Italian.

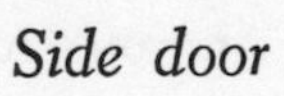

Side door

a few years ago) with such dazzling and stupefying brilliance is this: How to remain poor on a rich inheritance?

TIME

Everything in Italy is connected with the eternal sunshine. ("Eternal" here, as everywhere else, means frequent.) Things perish extremely quickly; light turns into darkness in no time; so one might as well take opportunities while they last. Be selfish, and keep your own interests in mind, but not too seriously. It is stupid, no doubt, to miss an opportunity; but, if it it missed, do not worry—another chance will come tomorrow. It is silly not to enjoy the sunshine, but, if you have something else to do, do it—you may be sure that the sun will shine again tomorrow. Sunshine is not a miracle in Italy; it is regarded as something almost natural.

Again, there is no need to hurry. The sun is eternal; Rome is eternal; and, if you miss one bus, another will follow. Time is not the fourth dimension in Italy; it is, indeed, the only commodity that is plentiful. "Time is money," say the Anglo-Saxons. If this saying were true, every Italian would be a millionaire. But time is money only for those who have not enough time. For the rest, time is not money; it has no value whatever.

"Half past eight tonight" in Italy means any time between ten P.M. and two A.M. If you have an appointment with someone at four o'clock and he turns up at half past six, he will not say, "Sorry I'm late." He is not late. There is no such thing in Italy as being late. He may ask you, as a matter of curiosity: "Have you been waiting long?" He wants to know whether you've been waiting five minutes or ten. It will never occur to him that, since your appointment was for four, you may have been waiting since four.

Nor is there any point in arranging a dinner party for Friday. Friday never comes. There is no such thing as Friday. Are you a fortune teller or a prophet to know at noon, on Monday, where you will be at 9:30 P.M. on Friday? Is it not a challenge and provocation to superior powers to make arrangements so far in advance? If you want to meet your friends on Friday, you call on Friday, and some will promise to come along, others will say they are busy. Now, discard those who promised to come; you certainly will not be seeing them. But, those who said that they could not possibly make it may turn up—oh, not at the suggested time and place, but somewhere else at another time. Since you are likely to have changed your rendezvous, too, you have every hope of a successful, indeed, roaring, party. I, at least, still have to see an Italian party which is not a roaring success.

If you want to meet a senior official in a ministry or the minister himself, just drop in at eight o'clock in the evening—unannounced, of course. They will be there, and they will see you. You will not find them in their office at 3:30 P.M.; at that time they are at home, fast asleep. Even eight o'clock may be a very bad time. You cannot be sure of finding your man. There is one way, however, of making pretty sure of not finding him: make an appointment. In England, an appointment is an engagement; in Italy, it is a fair warning of approaching danger.

Engagement diaries are unknown. The prime minister may have one, but junior ministers have never heard of the thing. Diaries are pompous articles. Only people with a sizable inferiority complex and those who mean to keep their engagements need engagement diaries. The Italians do not belong to either of these categories.

WOMEN

Are Italian women really beautiful? Yes, they are. Do they deserve their high reputation? Yes, they do. But then, of course, French, Hungarian, Swedish, English, and Spanish women are also beautiful—to say nothing of Greek, Irish, Portuguese, American, and Indian women. Women of all nationalities are beautiful—provided they are beautiful. I personally have a strong penchant for dark hair and dark eyes. So have all the Italians. It is lucky, indeed, that the Italians prefer Italian women, the English English women, the Bulgarians Bulgarian women, and that, generally speaking, every nation thinks its own women the most beautiful on earth. It would be extremely awkward if the French loved only Chilean women and South Africans only Finnish women.

Many people know only two things of the Italians—that their women are beautiful and that they eat macaroni. Few people are aware, however, of the disheartening connection between female beauty and macaroni. Excessive consumption of macaroni does not improve one's figure. This is the reason why one may see a fair number a beautiful Italian girls who—how shall put it?—remind you of sylphs only in a sitting position, but not when they walk in front of you in the street.

•

Are Italian women well dressed? Many of them are. Those who buy their clothes at the fashion designers of the Via dei Condotti are very well dressed indeed. Dior of Paris is not only a fashion king, he is a fashion himself; but one day he—and all the French designers with him—may be dethroned by the Italians.

There is a second category of Italian women, those who go to small dressmakers—a dying species in the West. These dressmakers work day and night in dingy rooms in bad light and charge very little for their unremitting labor. It is still the song of the shirt over there. They have taste and imagination; their clients have great beauty—more beauty than charm—and it is easy to dress them.

A large number of Italian women are not so well dressed. In fact, they go about in rags. The better-off women in this class wear neat rags; the poorer, torn and filthy rags.

Italy's clothing industry is about to enter a new stage. In England (and in many other countries), the cheap chain stores have created a revolution in female fashions. There are no longer any ragged women to be found there; everyone is well dressed, to the great sorrow of some people. "Uniformity" is, of course, frequently deplored; "lack of individuality" is found distressing. It hardly becomes me not to weep with the mourners. Lately it has become almost compulsory for writers —and especially for humorists—to strike a despondent attitude and lament the arrival of an era or horrid mass production. But this cannot be helped and, indeed, should be welcomed. General well-being implies a certain amount of uniformity. If all women started wearing original Schiaparelli models, it would still mean uniformity, all the same. Uniformity is simply a natural by-product of an industrial society—the alternative being picturesque, romantic, and very individual rags. Picturesque rags, however, are rather cold in the winter.

I know that many women heartily disagree with me. Many fight a desperate rearguard action against the idea that every salesgirl should have pretty, well-cut dresses and every factory girl an evening gown. Many rich women have enough poise, taste, and charm not to worry; others are driven to using more and more expensive materials, going to more and more exclusive tailors, and displaying larger and larger pieces of jewelry. It is true that men can hardly tell the difference between a $10 and $500 evening dress, but men are fools, and, in any case, women do not dress for the sake of men. Dowager duchesses and the wives of super-tax-paying executives (with a fair number of exemptions make a desperate effort to make themselves clearly distinguishable from factory girls and junior secretaries—which is a fatal mistake on their part. They would be well advised to spare no effort to resemble them.

This uniformity is, as yet, practically nonexistent in Italy —or at least in Southern Italy. It is just gaining a foothold. It is in the groping stage yet; the picturesque rag is still holding its own.

•

Italian girls are admirably (and, some wicked, wicked men would say, most regrettably) virtuous. The Roman Catholic

Church insists on a rigid standard of sexual morality, and poverty always places a high premium on virginity. In Italy, the Roman Catholic Church unites its forces with poverty. (This theory is logical; it is, alas, also untrue. The Americans attribute the same high value to virginity, but the United States is neither Catholic nor poor.)

Italians insist absolutely on a virgin bride, and the man who sent his newly wed wife back from their honeymoon and informed her parents by telegram: GOODS RETURNED—DAMAGED BEFORE DELIVERY may be exceptional in his forceful vulgarity, but the mentality reflected is general. A girl's virginity is her dowry, more often than not, her only dowry. Sexual morality is, of course, a matter of lofty principles; but it is also a matter of cash.

As a consequence of all this, Italian men in search of adventure are more likely to try their luck with married women than with girls. For the same reasons, a great many Italian novels avoid romantic—or any other—love and deal with marital problems instead.

•

Italy is still mainly a patriarchal society. The men often go out in the evening and leave their wives at home. They talk politics; the ladies talk kitchen, children, and dresses.

In every society where women are gently oppressed or kept in their place, they are also put on a pedestal. Here, again, the United States tends to spoil my theory by constituting an exception; there the men are oppressed, yet the women manage to cling to their pedestal. However, the Italian pedestal, in the middle and upper classes, is of a different kind. In this case, the women have not occupied the pedestal by force; they are put there for compensation. They stand on their pedestal, looking beautiful, wearing lovely clothes and a divine hair style—but they may speak only when spoken to.

Vespal virgin

4

BRITAIN
FRANCE
ITALY
√ GERMANY
SWITZERLAND
ISRAEL
JAPAN

THE GERMAN PROBLEM

I have been living with the German problem since my childhood. I was born in Hungary two years before the outbreak of World War I. I was about four or five when I heard my father say in the course of an argument: "No, you are mistaken. The Kaiser is not God. There is a great difference between God and the Kaiser. God knows everything; the Kaiser knows everything better." I knew very little about world politics then, but this sentence stuck clearly in my mind, where it built up a huge reputation for the Kaiser.

My next personal experience of the Germans brings me up to 1933. In that year, German Jewish refugees started pouring into Hungary, and a great number of them, mostly doctors, came to my father who—as was well known among the refugees—did what he could do for them and spent an immense amount of money in their aid. I remember one of them quite clearly, even today. He rang our bell at seven o'clock in the evening, and I opened the door to him. He looked like a thin man but was, in fact, a fat man grown thin. There was a strange look in his eyes. I thought it was fear; but it was hunger. He was hungry and was ashamed of it because people of his class and status did not go around hungry. At first sight, he looked neatly, almost well, dressed, but I noticed on closer examination that he was in rags. His clean and carefully pressed trousers were so worn that his bare knees showed when he sat down. One of the sleeves of his jacket had been torn but was carefully, almost invisibly, mended. And he had no socks on. All my father's patients had left, and he asked one of the maids to set a table in the waiting room and serve high tea for the visitor. I left them sitting talking.

When I returned half an hour later, the German doctor looked happier, and the hungry look had disappeared from his eyes. He was sitting in a deep armchair, smoking a cigarette. My father called in my grandfather and asked him to give a few pairs of socks to the German doctor. My grandfather—the mildest and most guileless of men—left and came back a few minutes later with four pairs of brand new socks. "Will striped ones do?" he asked the visitor politely, almost timidly. The visitor examined the socks before committing himself and then replied: "Well, if you haven't got anything else . . . but, quite frankly, I should prefer plain ones." There he was, terrified, hungry, and almost barefoot, and he would prefer plain socks to striped ones, free of charge. I thought it a capital joke. It was only many years later that I understood that it was no joke at all. It was the tragedy of the German character in a nutshell; it was the tragedy of the past eighty years condensed into four pairs of striped socks.

Then I thought a great deal about the Germans during the first Czechoslovak crisis in 1938, when I was traveling from Budapest to London. I thought a great deal about them when the house where I lived in 1940 was hit by a bomb. I pondered over the German problem when a flying bomb destroyed the Soho restaurant where I was having lunch one day in 1944 and my salad got so full of dust that I had to leave it, thus wasting ninepence.

I thought of the Germans very often when newsreels and documents about concentration camps and annihilation camps were released. And, a few years later, I, too, awaited their decision with breathless excitement: would they kindly allow us to rearm them?

But it was not these topical questions which really interested me. Why did these kindly and meditative souls go mad, start a planned war, and destroy millions of people with the cruelty of savages and the meticulous care of petty bureaucrats? Is there something inherently wrong in their character, or was it all a painful but—from the point of view of their character—unimportant incident, a regrettable misunderstanding? Do they know that they have blackened their names for a long time to come and that there are hundreds of thousands of people all over the world who hate and despise them and never want to set foot in Germany or talk to a German? Do they know this, and, if they do, what do they think about it? Is there a German problem for the Germans? Do they have a bad conscience and a guilt complex? Were they really Nazis? Are they Nazis today? What does it mean, anyway, to be a Nazi? Is every other German a murderer, as so many people seem to think? Or are they nice, honest, hard-working, kind men and women who may, however, kill another six million people if they get the chance?

To these questions I knew no answers. So, at the beginning of April, 1952, I descended into the depths of the German problem and did not emerge until the middle of May. I had never been in Germany before. Now I went there, armed with a couple of notebooks, a fountain pen, and two firm convictions:

Being anti-German is just as stupid a prejudice as being anti-Semitic, anti-Negro, or anti-American.

The right policy is to forgive but not to forget. And I

also knew that the policy followed by the West was to forget but not to forgive.

DUALISM

I found the general picture in Germany so confusing that I feel it is my duty to confuse the reader, too, right at the beginning; otherwise he may find it difficult or impossible to follow my line of argument.

Hitler was a naturalized German subject. He was the worst bargain in history. No other naturalized person has ever caused half so much trouble to his new fatherland. It is true that his naturalization followed a somewhat unusual pattern. Normally, it is the new subject who swears allegiance to the country; in Hitler's case, it was the country which swore allegiance to the new subject. That was a mistake. The English could have told the Germans that it never pays (1) to deviate from the tradition and (2) to trust foreigners too far.

Hitler was a great genius, and he succeeded in achieving the opposite of all his aims. He wanted to make Germany great; he made her small. He wanted to unite all Germans abroad; he succeeded in dividing even Germany proper into two. He wanted Germany to have colonies and succeeded in making Germany—for some time, at least—a colony herself. He was an amateur architect, wishing to build up a new and beautiful Germany as fast as possible, but he became the demolition expert who laid the whole country in ruins at record speed. He wanted to destroy Bolshevism and occupy Moscow. He destroyed Nazism instead and brought the Russian to Berlin and still farther west. He wanted to purify the German race, but today more white mothers have black children in Germany than anywhere else in the world. He wanted to make the Germans the master race and destroy the Jews; he was largely instrumental in establishing a new and independent Jewish state. You may say that all this is only the result of a lost

Dualism

war; but you may also say that all this is the natural and inevitable outcome of his activities.

Stalin in his German policy followed Hitler's example. He genuinely dreaded one thing—the rearmament of Germany. Consequently, he followed the one policy which did, in fact, bring about the realization of his fears.

All this has been a good lesson to the Western Allies, as well as to the Germans themselves. It is clearly silly to clamor and fight for one thing and then achieve its opposite. It is much more reasonable to fight for a certain aim and for its very opposite at one and the same time, and, whatever the outcome of the struggle, you get what you want. This Political Dualism is the new school now flourishing in London, Paris, Washington, and Bonn. Let us observe a few details of this policy. The Germans are too dangerous, so they must not build a new army, navy, air force or high command. But the Germans are on the western periphery of the Russian danger zone, and their country may be attacked, so they must take a hand in their country's defense. From these premises, the decision follows clearly: the Germans must be rearmed and kept disarmed at the same time. They must not be allowed to manufacture arms because they will soon outproduce the rest of Europe. But they must be forced to manufacture arms because otherwise they become too prosperous, and, free from the burden of rearmament, their competition will be ruinous for Britain. Whatever the Germans themselves want to do is sinister and suspicious. If they refuse to be rearmed, we say: "These wretched Germans! Of course, they want us to defend them and shed our blood for their safety." Should they, however, accept our invitation to rearm, then we exclaim: "These wretched Germans! Of course, they want to take advantage of this explosive situation. This is their first step toward rebuilding the *Wehrmacht*."

The West Germans have been under strong Western influences since the end of the war, and today they, too, think along the lines of Political Dualism. They want to rearm because it is essential that West Germany integrate with Western Europe, and the price of integration is rearmament. At the same time, they are reluctant to rearm because for them an army is synonymous with war, and the best way to avoid wars is to have no army. They want to be reunited with East Germany because this is the natural and honorable desire of every patriot. At the same time, they do not want to be reunited with East Germany because they fear, indeed, they know, that unity also means that sooner or later they will be swallowed up by the Soviet Union.

To sum up, Western statesmanship with the help of German ingenuity has succeeded, at last, in finding a generally accepted formula for the solution of the German question. The Germans must be rearmed and kept fully disarmed; German industry must produce war materials and must be absolutely forbidden to produce war materials. Germany should be reunited, but reunification must be prevented by all means. The British, French, and American forces must end the occupation of Germany, but they must stay in the country.

Without grasping these basic formulas no one can really understand the German problem and Western policy toward

Germany. I must ask the reader to keep this in mind, and then we may proceed to build up a general picture of the Germans and their fatherland.

THE DANGER OF WORKING

One of the greatest crimes of the Germans is that they work too hard. The English—quite rightly—can never forgive them this.

Even in 1952, a great part of Germany destroyed during the war had already been rebuilt. But the resulting picture was often a strange mixture of ruins and luxury. In Munich, the first thing which caught my eye was heaps of ruins, with hardly two stones on top of each other, but turned—not into dwelling houses or modest little shops—but into luxury establishments for selling porcelain and furs. Shop windows furnished with exquisite taste and packed with alluring treasures delighted your eyes; but you knew that a few corpses must still be buried under the ruins, just a few yards from the handbags, jewelry, and toys. Berlin's Kurfürstendamm had been rebuilt, but many of its houses were still uninhabitable, and some others empty shells only. The higher floor might still belong to the corpses; but the street level, with its treasures, luxurious goods, and dazzling neon lights, was a different story. Kurfürstendamm, though half of it was in ruins, was the richest and most beautiful shopping street in Europe.

It was perplexing, and you rubbed your eyes. "How to get defeated?" you asked yourself, in amusement or bitterness, depending on your temperament. There is a well-known story about two visitors from Israel talking about the situation in Germany. "I know what the solution is," says one of them. "It's all very simple. Israel ought to declare war on America." The other looks at him in some surprise. "Yes," the first one explains. "We should lose the war, and then the Americans would spend millions and millions on us. All our problems would be solved."

The other shakes his head sadly: "This is no solution."—"Why not?"—"Well," the other declares thoughtfully, "What if we beat America?"

The visitor from Israel was wrong. It was not Marshall aid which rebuilt Germany. Marshall aid undoubtedly helped—the gift of a few million dollars cannot do much harm to any country—but it was the amazing and staggering energy of the Germans which performed the miracles. Other countries, too, received Marshall aid, but no other country has achieved so much, although no other country (with the exception of certain parts of the Soviet Union) had to start building from scratch.

I stayed in a small *pension* in Berlin. A friend of mine had booked my room, and, when I arrived, at five o'clock on a Saturday afternoon, I found the whole place in an unholy mess. Workmen, bricklayers, decorators were rushing up and down; the furniture was hidden under white dust covers; masonry was falling everywhere while the noise of hammering and chiseling was deafening. I looked inquiringly at my friend, who explained, apologetically, that all this mess was a complete surprise to him. He had been living there for four weeks, and the building operations must have started only that morning, after he left at 8:30. I told him not to worry on my account; a little noise and dirt would not bother me in the least. Then I went to have a look at what the men were doing. A large room had been heavily damaged, and they had started rebuilding it. A few minutes later, my friend and I left the *pension* and did not return until two in the morning, when I saw the proprietress and two servants rushing busily hither and thither, carrying furniture and dragging carpets behind them along the corridor. I was tired, went to bed, and by next morning I had forgotten all about these activities. But my friend told me an amazing story. By midnight—and it was Saturday, as I have already mentioned—the builders and decorators had finished their work, and then the proprietress and the two maids started scrubbing the floor, cleaning and furnishing the room, and went on working until 3 A.M. At eight o'clock on Sunday morning, the room was occupied by a married couple with a child, and it looked spotlessly clean and very comfortable. This tempo was miraculous. In England, the same work would have lasted for weeks. But in Germany it seemed to be normal and natural, maybe even on the slowish side.

It was not only building and rebuilding which was pursued with such energy. I saw many waiters in restaurants at two in the morning and met the same waiters again at eight, serving breakfast. I admire the German tempo; let me add in fairness to ourselves that I, for one, prefer to be turned out from a restaurant at 11 P.M. in the knowledge that the waiters will have their proper rest.

In Bavaria, Berlin, and Hesse, I saw people work until midnight—not only waiters, but also bricklayers and decorators. I saw others working as early as four in the morning. Yet, all these people jibe at the Swabians. "Oh, those Swabians," they keep saying. "They work too hard." I visited Stuttgart, but failed to detect anything to distinguish the way the Swabians work from the way the rest of Germany works. Perhaps they work twenty-eight hours a day; I could not find out.

I personally have nothing against work. Many people from Marcus Aurelius to Tolstoy—in other words, people who worked very little in their lives in the ordinary sense of the word—found labor beautiful and exhilarating and exhorted others to work hard. Carlyle was more logical. Sometimes he found work bliss; on other occasions, a nuisance. In *Past and Present*, he wrote: "Blessed is he who has found his work; let him ask no other blessedness." But, in *The Nigger Question*, he declared: "Labor is not joyous, but grievous." And Carlyle was right. Work is sometimes bliss, sometimes—much more often—a confounded nuisance. I think that it is silly to preach to people that they should work because work is pure joy. They should work because labor earns happiness and leisure, and there is, unfortunately, no other way of earning them. To tell a man that his work is a pleasure for him is the same as informing him that you do not appreciate his labor. You do not appreciate a person for enjoying himself. Luckily, few people will believe that carrying heavy sacks, cleaning offices, and adding up long columns is the greatest blessedness. We all have to work, however, and some are luckier in their work than others. A few, again, really love and enjoy it. Longfellow wrote: "Learn to labor and to wait." The Germans learned to labor; the British learned to wait. A fair distribution of labor. The Germans have my admiration; the British, all my sympathy. You must be careful with work. You can overdo it. The trouble with work is that it grows on you. The more you work, the more you are willing to work. It may become quite a habit. I am sure that that is what has happened to the Germans. Ever since I reached the age of twenty-five, I have wanted to retire. All Frenchmen, too, look forward to their retirement with expectation and gusto. The Germans dread it. For the French, life begins when working ends; for the Germans, when the working days end, life itself comes to an end, too.

One of these industrious Germans told me, with every sign of self-pity, that their habit of working hard made them unpopular. "Between the two wars," he told me, "we arrived in China and changed everybody's habits. Before we came, the English shipping firms had had a monopoly. They went to their offices at eleven-thirty, mostly to do nothing. After lunch, they hardly ever returned. Mail boats arrived once a month; so about once a month they prepared all their mail and spent the rest of their time playing golf and drinking whisky. After our arrival, they had to work like slaves. They had to open their offices at eight and keep them open until seven in the evening if they did not want to lose all their clients. And they did not like us. Just because we worked hard."

He sighed: "The world doesn't understand us."

I looked at him and then said one word: "Disgusting."

He nodded. But, a few seconds later, his face darkened. He could not be quite sure that my remark referred to the world which did not understand him.

The danger of German humor

THE DANGER OF GERMAN HUMOR

The German lack of a sense of humor has created two world wars.

This is not a sweeping statement, but a sober assessment of historical truth.

We are inclined to say that a person has no sense of humor if he (1) does not laugh at our jokes and (2) laughs at things at which we do not, just as we call a man ill-mannered if he follows a different code of etiquette from ours. The Mundugumor tribe of New Guinea, for instance, eat human flesh—which we do not—and we condemn their habits; but, on the other hand, they eat very little other meat, so they, in turn, disapprove of us. Who is right? I do not pretend to know. But we cannot do better in matters relating to manners, sense of humor, and ethics than to abide by our own standards, as we, indeed, always do.

A lot of beautiful things have been said about a sense of

humor. It is a wonderful thing, people keep repeating; it makes one man much more valuable than his neighbor who lacks it. Such statements usually mean that the speaker, who has an exquisite sense of humor—the speaker always has—regards himself as a wonderful man, much better than his neighbor. But a sense of humor may be a good or bad characteristic. A person who is too ironic—however witty he may be—is often only a coward. He knows that he is a constant loser on the so-called battlefields of life and tries to console himself by laughing at love and beauty. That is why the Anglo-Saxons are so right in distrusting irony. Irony, on some occasions, may be an effective and justified weapon in the fight against wickedness, selfishness, and stupidity; but in other cases it may only be the parting arrow of an inferior warrior with which he tries to assert his nonexistent superiority. Even the admirable ability to laugh at ourselves is often nothing but inverted conceit. You are right in enjoying a good sense of humor, but be careful in admiring it. I am all against it. It makes me suspicious. I dislike humorists, especially good ones.

A good sense of humor—whatever its psychological origin—is the ability to see life in a rosier light. It may make one happier, but this is one's private affair. The only general importance of a sense of humor is the fact that it goes with a sense of proportion. It either produces a sense of proportion or is produced by it. If we have a sense of humor, we cannot consider our affairs terribly and overwhelmingly important. Of course, we all know that we are wonderful creatures, but our self-admiration is at least tempered by the knowledge that we have minor faults. Yes, we are noble, unselfish, dignified (but not pompous), goodhearted, brilliantly intelligent, and extremely capable in almost everything; but we are ready to admit that we do not know the railway timetable by heart. An average German would never admit this. I heard long, heated, and acrimonious arguments about whether, on a certain journey, one had to change at Heidelberg. Both sides used weighty and convincing arguments (except the timetable itself), and the losers, in the end, felt genuinely angry and resentful.

Dictatorship and the lack of a sense of humor go hand in hand because the admiration of a dictator or an infallible party presupposes lack of a sense of proportion. People say that a totalitarian system could not gain foothold in Britain or in the United States because these countries have long democratic traditions. This is a mistake. A totalitarian system can be enforced by bayonets, and traditions have very little to do with it —although traditions may compel the bayonets to do a more ruthless job. The Czechs used to have democratic traditions. But listen once to a Czech telling you a funny story, and you will fell anxiety for their country. A dictator would have great difficulty in Britain because the British would laugh at him. An Englishman loves his country, but he would never speak of "the beloved and blood-soaked Fatherland of my glorious ancestors." If someone else did in his presence, he would cast his eyes down and feel uncomfortable; and, two hours later—at home—he would laugh. Speak in England of "blood and soil," and people will roar their heads off. In Britain, excessive sycophancy, whenever it occurs—and it occurs sometimes—is often pilloried and ridiculed. Hitler and Stalin made gods of themselves in Germany and Russia; they would have made fools of themselves here. A dictator in Britain probably could not be chased away today, since the central power wielded by any government has become too strong for rebellion; but it could be laughed away. Before the war, whenever German troops were seen goose-stepping on British newsreels, the audience was always amused and laughed loudly. In Germany, the goose-step was found most impressive; the English thought it was done only to amuse them. Throughout the war, I was haunted by the thought that the Germans might use it in a major battle. The British—I feared —would instantly drop their guns and steel helmets and lie around helpless with laughter. Had the Germans tried that, they might have won the Battle of Alamein. It is lucky that Rommel never thought of it. But, even if he had thought of it, he would never have tried it. The goose-step was sacred—not to be made fun of. German generals preferred losing the Battle of Alamein.

Not that the Germans do not laugh a great deal. But observe their pleasure and their merriment. The *Bräu* (the *Bierhalle*, or tavern) often looks like a temple, with its massive Gothic arches. There sit the Germans—with scars on their faces—not simply eating and drinking gallons of beer and yards of sausages but making sacrifices to Bacchus and to the god of Good Appetite. The mood is solemn. A man must occasionally enjoy himself, and they are performing a duty now. Along the walls are little statues on tiny shelves, who all represent saints in the temple—Bacchanalian saints, but saints all the same. One little statue in a Bavarian city is the image of a fat little man who is being sick, having drunk too much beer, and is now holding his forehead and vomiting into his hat. This is supposed to be a joke, and a very funny joke at that. It is, in fact, one of the sights of that famous city. The waitressess of the *Bräu* are dressed in gay yellow and green—they usually have enormous bosoms—and their friendly smiles express approval of your eating and drinking a lot. But, primarily, they do not serve you; they serve higher and gayer masters, the pagan gods and saints on the wall. The Germans eat and drink industriously and conscientiously under the Gothic arches in the shadow of grinning and vomiting statues and go home after midnight with the gratifying feeling that their duty has been done.

And, of course, they laugh, too. But the question is not so much *at what* as *when?* It rather depends on the calendar. Every German knows that the time of the October festivals and the times of *Fasching* (carnival time) are times of gaiety. They know for months beforehand that, let us say, on October 3, they will be hilariously happy. They go out to the October festival and have a jolly good time because they have made a note of it in their diary months before. And then they really let themselves go. They shriek and shout. They sit next to one another, singing songs, rocking rhythmically, drinking beer by the gallon, and roasting whole oxen in one piece—one single, colossal joint. The joke is that someone is fat and ugly and dances comically, with a fatuous smile on his face. The joke is that he falls on his behind. The joke is that the musicians are also enormously fat, that they wear tiny bowler hats on their big round heads and play so loudly that no one can hear even his own voice. Strangers dance with one another, strangers kiss one another and smack one another on certain parts of the body where they find, as a rule, plenty of surface for smacking. During the carnival parade, the shop windows of Cologne have to be boarded up, otherwise they would be smashed—not through wickedness, not with malice, only as a joke. All this is not very subtle. They are not Voltaire's spiritual descendants, but their laughter is robust and healthy. Of course, there are many truly witty and enchanting people in Germany, just as anywhere else, but, however large their number may be, they are not characteristic of the community. The beer festivals and carnival parades are characteristic. The fat man who falls on his back and is greeted by uproarious laughter is characteristic. Humorists may not be the cream of humanity; or, again, they may. Whatever the case, it is significant that the Germans have produced so very few good humorists. They produce literary giants, like Thomas Mann for one, but he has hardly written two lines which are considered even faintly humorous outside Germany.

Berlin is an exception. Berliners are the only Germans I have met who have a sense of humor in our meaning of the word. Their sense of humor is a little cruel; it is mingled with *Schadenfreude*, often against themselves. Yet, they have the above-mentioned ability to laugh at themselves. At the time of the heaviest air raids, the Berliner—and he alone among the Germans—was able to look around his destroyed city and, hearing the scream of a new air raid warning, remark, looking up at the sky: "But now they have to bring the house with them too." Berliners are very different in many ways from the rest of the people. The isolation of Berlin from the rest of Germany is not only geographical; it is also symbolic.

Historical materialism, although containing more than a grain of truth, has its weak sides, too. Historical humorism—a new science, just invented—is much safer. A great power on the plain—I mean geographically, without natural frontiers—tends to lose its sense of humor, and this is the source of all evil. But the great power on the plain may also lose its great power and the plain itself. So it may learn. I, as the founder of historical humorism, if I may take my modest bow, will not only admire but also sincerely love the Germans as soon as they produce their own, original Edward Lear. Show me the first utterly nonsensical and truly popular limerick in German, and I, for one, shall exclaim with joy: "The German danger has passed forever!"

I have no idea, of course, how the Germans will take this chapter. It would be utterly unfair on my part to suggest that, should they dislike and reject it, that would be a proof, or a further proof, of their lack of a sense of humor. They may possess the most exquisite sense of humor and still dislike and condemn my book for a number of well-founded reasons. But, while in Germany, I was often asked a question by various people which I found surprising. They would discuss with me the book I was planning on Germany and then ask me in a voice betraying surprise, hope, and incredulity: "But you do not want to write this book in your own style?"

I sighed deeply and replied: "Not really. But the trouble is, you see, that I have no choice."

ON THE SCARCITY OF TEUTONIC GODS

Suppose that you want to become a German.

You need not be a Teutonic god. You need not be six feet tall, broad-shouldered, fair, blue-eyed or divine in any particular way. If your laugh chimes melodiously like church bells sunk in the Rhine, that is all right; but, if it happens to be an uproarious belly laugh, do not worry. If you are brave and vengeful like Siegfried, good for you; but, if you are meek and humble, that will do as well. If you are lean and muscular like the war-

On the scarcity of Teutonic gods

riors of the Nibelungenlied, that must be good for your health; but, if your girth borders on the miraculous and you have a treble chin as well as a treble neck, you are still eligible.

Go and have a haircut. Most people have an ordinary, European haircut, but a large minority—I always felt that only they were the true Germans—have their hair shorn off completely, except for a fetching little mane just above the forehead. Then dress up. Dress like a hunter, but never go hunting or as a golfer but never play golf. Once I saw a whole orchestra in a night club wearing shorts and hunters' jackets, and I was told that they were Bavarian peasants. Later I saw Bavarian peasants dressed as golfers, and I was told that they were hunters.

Whatever you do, be stiff and formal like a foreign ambassador performing an official duty. I have always believed that "charm" often conceals a streak of weakness. The majority of Germans are completely free of this weakness. Titles are never dropped; if you are addressing someone 238 times in the course of an evening, give him his full title 238 times. And, if you go on meeting him for fifty years, give him his full title for fifty years. I visited the house (bombed and rebuilt) in Frankfurt where Goethe was born, and the guide always referred to Goethe's father as the *Herr Rat* (Mr. Councilor). Not once did he allow himself more familiarity with a man who has been dead for about 200 years. If a man happens to have two degrees, call him *Herr Doktor Doktor*. One *Herr* will do, but you must say *Doktor* twice. I thought this was a joke, and not even a good one, until I saw "Dr. Dr." written on the doors of numerous officials.

Be decent, well-meaning, and clean, and believe that cleanliness is one of the greatest of human virtues. Look down on the French because some—in fact many—of their lavatories are dirty. The French, to my mind, are one of the most brilliant and lovable peoples in the world, and even their lavatories belong to the great blessings of humanity. Millions of people may feel superior to them because their lavatories are cleaner than those of the French. I, personally, have a bias for dirt. Not too much dirt—I am moderate in my tastes—but a little dirt. I laugh at the man who spends half an hour a day polishing his shoes and four hours every Saturday afternoon cleaning his car. I like shoes and cars clean if someone else cleans them; but I prefer them slightly dirty if I have to clean them myself. But I shall never make a good German.

Always be well dressed whether you are a millionaire or a beggar. Frenchmen spend most of their money on food and drinks and do not care how they are dressed; the Germans would sooner go around hungry—as many of them do—but they are always presentably dressed. In Germany, few people would give money to a poorly clad beggar.

Always explain the obvious, and explain it with a dogmatic air as if you had just discovered, for the first time in the history of human thought, that two and two make four, that birds fly in the air, and that trains are sometimes late.

Be highly cultured, quote Greek authors in the original, be interested in everything, and amass a huge volume of factual information. If you have a chance—and you will often find one if you are on your guard—air your vast knowledge just to show that you possess it. Be paternal to everybody, and teach everybody his own business. Do this benevolently, full of the noblest intentions and with the tact of a baby elephant. In Berlin, I deposited all my cash and travelers' checks with the *pension*-keeper, because I hate carrying much money on me (thank Heavens, I am not exposed too often to this inconvenience). Next day, needing more money, I asked the lady for some. Instead of handing over my envelope, she asked me: "How much?" "Fifty marks," I said; "it's for one day only." She opened the envelope and gave me forty marks. "Forty is quite enough for one day," she said, a little brusquely. I did not dare to argue. It *was* enough; she was right. She saved me ten marks. You could have deposited with her (or with ninety-nine Germans out of a hundred) a huge fortune, uncounted. They are honest and reliable. You would get your money back to the last *pfennig*—if only you could pluck up enough courage to ask for it.

LOVE THY NEIGHBOR

I had a conversation with a German policeman at Mannheim, near the Rhine bridge. I do not think that one could have a similar conversation with a policeman of any other nationality. He was a young man, with large blue eyes and wide Teutonic features, good-looking in a very German way. He stopped me because of my headlights. The streets were rather dark in this particular place, and, in addition to my sidelights, I had my headlights on, properly dimmed. Certain English cars—for some unknown and to me completely mysterious reason—are so constructed that, when you dim your headlights, one of them goes off altogether. The car looks like a one-eyed giant, a modern Cyclops; what is much worse, from a distance it looks like a motorcycle. My policeman, too, was surprised to see that I turned out to be a car.

"One of your headlights is off," he said.

"I know," I replied. "I am sorry, but my car is constructed that way."

"That I don't believe," he said, with engaging straightforwardness

"That is extremely sad," I answered. "And I cannot prove it either."

"Why should they build cars that way?" he inquired.

"I have no idea. Probably for reasons of economy."

"But they can't economize like that," he said, and I believe he was right.

"Doesn't that strike you as quite senseless?" he asked.

"It does."

"Then why do they do it?"

"I can't tell you. I should love to, but I really can't. I should say as a guess, since in England we drive on the left side of the road, it is sufficient to light up the pavement side."

"That is quite logical," he nodded.

"But you said it was quite senseless," I reproved him.

"And you agreed."

He had me there.

"However you build your cars in England," he continued, "in Germany you should have two dimmed headlights. If you come to this country you should comply with the regulations."

"I fully agree. You are right. But do the regulations say that you must have two dimmed lights or only that you may?"

He was a bit perplexed and did not answer. I tried to follow up my advantage:

"Anyway, I have been here only a short time, and I am going to leave soon."

"Oh—you have not been here long . . . ?"

"No."

"Then how is it that you speak German so well?"

It was the first time anyone had told me that, but I did not argue the point.

"I learned it a long time ago, in Vienna."

"When?"

"About twenty years ago."

"'What did you do in Vienna?"

Love thy neighbor

"I was studying."

"What?"

It began to sound like a cross-examination.

"It is no secret at all, but I can't quite see what it has to do with my headlights."

He was very much annoyed.

"You must have your headlights seen to."

"I shan't."

"But you have to."

"I know. But I shan't."

He did not know how to take that. A long pause followed; then he asked: "Then what can I do?"

"Nothing," I replied.

"You mean nothing at all?"

"Absolutely nothing at all," I nodded. "Unless, of course, you wish to take me to the police station."

"I can't do that," he shook his head. "We are instructed to show the utmost leniency to foreign motorists."

"Well, then show it," I told him, switching on my most disarming Central-European smile.

He saluted and let me pass.

I rather enjoyed that conversation. He showed a large amount of common sense mingled with the same amount of naïveté. His willingness to let me pass was not simply because he could not be bothered with such a trifle; he let me pass in the end because he remembered an instruction which fitted the situation. If it was his duty to "be lenient"; that was quite a different proposition. Life is full of problems, if you know how to find them.

I also liked the engaging honesty of a *Würstlerei* owner in Munich. A *Würstlerei* is a place where you can get sausages and beer and nothing else. Now, the Germans, especially the Southern Germans, are the greatest sausage-makers in the world, and I am the most outstanding sausage-connoisseur who ever trod this planet. I could never pass any of these establishments without dashing in to eat a pair of sausages and drink a glass of beer—although my figure, even as it is, leaves much to be desired. This particular *Würstlerei* consisted of one tiny room with a few chairs and some boards running along the wall so that you could place your plate and glass on them. The walls were covered with nudes and other beauties advertising various makes of beer. I was admiring the beauties when my eye caught a small notice which read: "*Toilette* in the Café Speizmann, next door, in the basement."

I was deeply touched by this. It was the last degree of honesty, I thought, to draw all the customers' attention to the fact that they had no *toilette* there. It was even more honest to point out that even the nearest *toilette*—in the Café Speizmann—was in the basement. But that little notice meant even more than that. It was the shining example of cooperation and unselfishness. Why not let the Café Speizmann have a share in the business? A fair distribution of the benefits of a blooming concern, I reflected. That is what the Germans rightly call *leben und leben lassen*—to live and let live.

RACIAL HATRED

It is enough to spend a few days in Germany to notice that almost everybody is something different from what he used to be. The university professor has turned businessman, and the army officer has just come back to Germany from Addis Ababa, where he is agricultural adviser to the emperor. The former teacher has turned haulage contractor, and the former banker is now a geologist. This professional upheaval is the outcome of a mass movement of people. Thanks to the war, Germany is full of refugees, and this is the cause of countless individual tragedies, as well as economic difficulties. Huge masses were evicted from the provinces occupied by the Russians and Poles; hundreds of thousands escaped from the East before and after the Russians arrived; further hundreds of thousands were expelled from Central European and Balkan countries, where many of them behaved abominably during Hitler's heyday and were subsequently made to pay for their crimes. But not only the guilty were punished, the innocent, indeed, the loyal and faithful suffered as well. The very first man I met in Germany—a gentleman of about sixty who looked like a hunter, to whom I gave a lift after crossing the border at Lindau—had lived all his life in Maribor, Yugoslavia. Now he was living in Baden and was on a temporary visit in Bavaria, but his family had originally come from Hamburg. You may stop someone in a Munich street to ask the way and it is as likely as not that the reply will be in a Silesian, East Prussian, or Berlin dialect. All this is the source of a great deal of racial hatred or at least impatience. The refugees consider themselves victims of the war, which indeed they are.

The difference between the various Germans—people from Baden, Bavaria, Prussia, Hamburg, Saxony, Hessen, Westphalia, the Rhineland, Württemberg, East Prussia, etc.—is said to be considerable. The Prussians are of Slav descent; the others are Teutons. Their history and environment differ, and their traditions vary to a great extent. I do not know the various German

Racial hatred

races well enough to paint portraits of them, and I do not think it would be worthwhile repeating the well-known truisms about Prussian militarism, Swabian diligence, Bavarian slowness, and all the other clichés. I wish to make only two remarks in this connection.

(1) It is probably a favorable turn of events that German race hatred, or animosity, is turned against other Germans. This animosity is not very dangerous, after all, and whenever it becomes dangerous it is controlled by reason and legislation. But the Germans seem to be in need of discharging a certain amount of race hatred, just as a car must discharge poisonous gases. It is much better if they discharge these gases on the home market. I am convinced that the Swiss have succeeded in behaving like civilized human beings and living in peace with the rest of the world for such a long time largely because they have the courage to dislike and even detest one another.

(2) It is probably true that Prussians are rude and rough. And Prussian militarism—a justified charge—is the crux of the matter. But I rather like them for their rudeness. Roughness and rudeness may arise from various psychological factors, but one of them surely is a trait of honesty and outspokenness. I have always found Prussians honest and straightforward. Too straightforward, if anything. After all, hypocrisy and flattery

may have their points, and courtesy could be defended by skillful arguments; but straightforwardness, too, has some inherent merits. And anybody who knows Berlin will agree that Prussian Jews are not different from Prussian Christians. Kinder people regard this fact as going to prove the utter silliness of race theories. Less kind people will simply remark that Prussian Jews unite Prussian charm with Jewish modesty.

5

BRITAIN
FRANCE
ITALY
GERMANY
√ SWITZERLAND
ISRAEL
JAPAN

THE LARGEST COUNTRY IN THE WORLD

One of the best-guarded secrets of the Swiss is that there are really no such people. There are no Swiss. The outside world may be misled by superficial external appearances; the Swiss themselves—for reasons of policy, diplomacy, and also because it would be too complicated to explain all this to dense foreigners—refrain from pricking the legend and behave as though they existed. But they do not.

Looking at the map, you might easily jump to the conclusion that the United States is a larger country than Switzerland. Wrong again. It is much smaller. This is one of the reasons why you can speak of "Americans," but you cannot really speak of "the Swiss." In the United States, quite a lot of people—whether from the Wild West (Oregon) or the Wild East (New York), from the Deep South (Georgia) or the Deep North (Michigan)—are prepared to call themselves "Americans."* There is a legend (which plenty of songs and poems try to keep alive) that America does something peculiar to your soul. Well, it certainly does; but it does not transform a Central European bank clerk, a Negro witch doctor, a Syrian bookmaker, a Japanese wrestler, a Sicilian tourist guide, and a Scandinavian sailor, in no time, into that instantly recognizable, wonderful, and unique paragon of humanity, the *Homo americanus*, as they are so fond of maintaining. The Swiss know better. It is not only that the Swiss French will have nothing to do with the Swiss Germans, whereas neither of them will have anything to do with the Swiss Italians—life is never quite so simple as that. But ask a man of Lausanne what he thinks of the people of Geneva; ask the same man of Lausanne whether he likes the people of Berne; ask a man of Basle if he would like to be taken for a man from Zürich; ask a man of Chur, in eastern Switzerland, whether he feels himself nearer to the man in the Moon or to a man from St. Gallen. There is a saying that there are three qualifications any bishop of Chur may possess: (1) he must be a Roman Catholic, (2) he must be a consecrated priest, and (3) he must be a native of Chur or, least, of the canton of Graubunden. But—people like to add—the first two requirements might be dispensed with.

I once knew a charming old gentleman, a prominent manufacturer in one of the three original cantons, who had classified all his compatriots very precisely. He would never employ a man from Appenzell (forty-three miles northeast of his village), because people from Appenzell are "impertinent and mean." People coming from about twenty-five miles south of Appenzell—the people of the Grisons or Graubunden—though quite different, were not much better, because, though they were certainly capable, they were utterly unreliable. People from about thirteen miles to the north of Appenzell—the people of St. Gallen—were quite different again, in fact people from another

* There are, of course, no such people as "the British," either. A man is an Englishman or a Scotsman, a Welshman or an Irishman; only newly naturalized people would describe themselves as British; and the Americans talk of the British.

planet, but they were of no use at all, either, because they were lazy. People of Berne were too slow-witted, and people from Lucerne too weak and irremediably spoiled by the tourists. In short, no people were any good at all, except those from his immediate neighborhood, who, however, were all rotters anyway and not to be touched with a ten-foot pole. When his son —who was also his general manager—married, he moved out of the paternal home and went to live with his wife in Zug, about twelve miles away (but in another canton), whence he drove daily to his job in his father's factory. After eighteen months, his father managed not only to quarrel with him, but also to drive him out of his job. The son is convinced that the real reason for this break was his father's deep and unalterable conviction that the "people of Zug are petty and calculating."

This ethnic variety, these irreconcilable differences between the people of Appenzell and those of Schwyz (divided from each other by forty-three infinite miles), between the people of Zug and those of Winterthur, make Switzerland one of the largest countries in the world. This mutual dislike, contempt, and healthy detestation of one another is the really firm foundation of Swiss democracy and neutrality. "Love thy neighbor," says the Christian teaching, and a profound and noble teaching it certainly is. But loving Christians fought each other for thirty years in a devastating and cruel war in the seventeenth century and, indeed, during long centuries before and ever since. No, you cannot love someone if you simply detest him. Ask any man of Basle if he could possibly love a man of Zürich; ask a man of Olten if he could possibly love a man of Aarau. You cannot love him, but you can *tolerate* him. And love, if not sincere, is hypocrisy; *tolerance* is the shining democratic virtue. For people of Basle to tolerate the people of Zürich as neighbors is incredible self-discipline; for the people of Uri to live in peaceful coexistence with that impertinent and mean lot at Appenzell is a great and admirable achievement; for the people of Lausanne to restrain themselves and start no wars of revenge against the Bernese, who once invaded and subjugated them, is the pinnacle of civilized self-control. I knew a lady in Schaffhausen, the watchmakers' town, whose son married a girl from Winterthur —about fifteen miles away. She was heartbroken, of course, and explained to me in great confidence that she was making a great effort to treat her daughter-in-law "as though she were one of us," although she knew very well that these "mixed marriages never worked." She, too, regarded herself as a miracle of self-sacrifice and almost superhuman self-control.

And that is the whole point. The human soul needs to get rid of a certain amount of hatred and nastiness, just as an internal combustion engine must get rid of a certain amount of poisonous gas. The Swiss get rid of these gases by despising each other so intensely that they have no energy to spare for hating the rest of humanity. Look at Germany, to mention only one example; since her unification, she has plunged the world into two world wars. It seems clear that the original unification of Germany was bad luck for humanity. And humanity hardly knows how lucky it is that there is no hope and not the faintest chance whatsoever of bringing about the unification of Switzerland.

JUST LUCK

I have a charming and extremely talented relative who is something of a mathematical genius and, on top of it, one of the most modest persons I know. He has never regarded any achievement of his as really his; it was "just luck." In fact, there was a time when I used to address him as "Just Luck." It was just luck when, at the age of twenty, he was offered so many scholarships at Princeton University that he had to decline some; it was simply not worthwhile taking them because his income tax would have run too high. It was also just luck when, at the age of twenty-one, during the war, he was sent to Los Alamos to do very responsible work on the atomic bomb. He had good luck again when he was appointed assistant to Albert

Einstein; it was just luck when he became a full professor at Princeton University in his late twenties; and he had further luck when, just under thirty, he became head of the mathematics department of another famous American university with some thirteen professors working under him. It was just luck, he said earnestly, and I believe that he meant it.

I am reminded of this attitude when I hear people say that Switzerland is so lucky to possess all that natural beauty. To some extent, she certainly is; no human endeavor or devotion could make Saudi Arabia half as beautiful. But a great deal of Switzerland is man-made beauty. They make the best of nature's gifts. Austria or Yugoslavia could be just as beautiful; all nature's gifts are there. For some people, indeed, Switzerland is too elaborate, and a minority prefer Austria or Yugoslavia, on the grounds that their beauty is more natural and unspoiled. But this "elaboration" is not luck; it is the result of much work. Switzerland may be "spoiled" for some, but all that "spoiling" is the result of hard work. It may be ridiculous to find a hotel on every mountain top and "Pass Höhe," but it is not "just luck" that the hotels are there. They were built there. It may be amusing to see innumerable ski lifts and *Seilbahnen* and funiculars all over the place, but ski lifts and the rest do not grow like fir trees; they have to be produced by a certain artificial method.

The Swiss are, indeed, hard-working people, and this devotion to work is one of their most repulsive virtues. Altogether, it is the virtues of the Swiss which I find a bit hard to bear. Coming from England, I regard work as some sort of nuisance you must pretend to be engaged in between cups of tea. But the Swiss take work seriously—start early, finish late, and are even proud of it. They are paid for it handsomely—more handsomely than the English—and their old-fashioned idea is that they ought to play fair. The employer is not simply the chap you organize strikes against; he must pay, to be sure, and pay a lot, but he must also receive value for his money. This attitude is, of course, quite outmoded in the second half of the twentieth century.

Another Swiss virtue that tends to drive me slightly crazy is their kindness and politeness. I am speaking now of German Switzerland only. Whatever is going on—in an office, in a shop, in a restaurant, in any field of private life—they keep on saying *Bitte schön* almost endlessly, to which you are supposed to reply *Danke schön.* Should you stop this exchange of *Bitte schön–Danke schön* before twenty-two rounds are up (and with a few exclamations of *Ja, gerne* thrown in), you are regarded as an uncivilized barbarian. I have seen people drop with exhaustion, and their last words before passing out completely were a few whispered *Danke schöns* or *Bitte schöns.* You have to say *Grütsi* to all and sundry all the time. This is a Swiss greeting, and you cannot say it often enough. You do not really say it, you sing it. When you meet several people, you say, *Grütsi miteinander* . . . or something like that and it sounds like a whole operatic aria from the mouth of any true-born Swiss. In wild mountain passes, everyone you meet will sing *Grütsi* to you. You sing *Grütsi* to them and exchange, if you have any manners at all, a few *Danke schöns* and *Bitte schöns.* You will be quite hoarse by the time you part. Once, near Interlaken, I was walking alone in the mountains of the Bernese Oberland when I saw a solitary cow coming toward me. She stopped. I stepped out of her way, but she did not move. She went on looking at me with her sad brown eyes. There we were, the cow and I; neither of us would move. I was nonplussed. At last, after two or three minutes, I said, *Grütsi.* She nodded to me seriously and walked on.

The honesty of the Swiss is not easy to bear, either. I do not insist on being diddled as one is diddled fifty times a day in Venice or Naples. I can do without that reasonably well. I do not mind if, in restaurants, I know that there is no need to check up on checks because it is unlikely that the waitress has added the date to the check. But there comes a point where you feel that honesty has gone a little too far. Too much shining honesty tends to blind you a little. A year or two ago, my wife and I went into a shop that had a number of electric irons displayed in the window to see whether we could leave a few things to be cleaned and ironed. It turned out, however, that the shop was not a cleaner's but a place where they sold electric irons. "Sorry," we said and turned to leave. The lady behind the counter, unwilling to see us disappointed, offered to lend us an iron for a day or two. My wife accepted gladly; how much did we pay for it? Oh, nothing, the lady said, there was no charge. My wife then offered to leave a deposit, which the lady refused. My wife then wanted to leave our name and address at least—at which I dragged her out of the shop and fled. I realized that the shopkeeper lady was getting suspicious and had started looking at us as though we were habitual criminals—the ideas we had! The fact that we were offering deposits and trying to leave our names and address clearly proved that we were the kind of people to whom the *possibility* had occurred that an electric iron might be stolen. This was indeed suspicious. I took to my heels because I was afraid that she might call the police.

But cleanliness is the most terrifying of all Swiss virtues. When you go on making jokes for years about the Swiss vacuuming their roads between villages, and then, one day, you actually see a vast electric vacuum cleaner cleaning the open road, then you say to yourself that this mania for cleanliness has got out of hand. When you realize that a road-sweeper or a garbage collector is actually cleaner in Switzerland than many a waiter in certain other countries, then you start longing for just a little dirt here and there.

This problem has, however, its glorious side, too. The Swiss have, in fact, solved the perennial question which has troubled philosophers throughout the centuries: What is the aim of life? The answer the Swiss give to this question is simple, original, and convincing: the aim of life is to make your door knob shine.

DEMOCRACY WITH A SCHWITZERDUTSCH ACCENT

If it is not easy to forgive the virtues of the Swiss, they do luckily possess some redeeming sins which endear them to all of us.

The first case to mention is the Swiss version of democracy, which is democracy with a strong *Schwitzerdutsch* accent. The constitution evolved from the pact of 1291; nevertheless, this shining example of a democratic state leaves half its citizens disenfranchised. I speak, of course, of the women. A few cantons have recently given women the right to vote, but women do not possess the *federal* vote, nor do they seem to be worried by this. There is a movement to get the vote for women, but it is not really strong or highly vociferous, and it compares to the suffragette movement in pre-World War I Britain rather as that war itself compares to a village brawl. Swiss women, on the whole, do not want the vote. They prefer life in a political ghetto, and the walls of all the ghettos of this world, after an initial period of confusion and revolt, are always defended from within. It is often not easy to get out of the ghetto; but it is always much more difficult to get in. Why are Swiss women content to leave politics to their men? There are many reasons, and I will mention only three of them—the less obvious ones.

(1) The Swiss, though passionately interested in other people's politics, do not get overexcited about their own. The Swiss are great newspaper-readers, and their small country has some of the greatest newspapers in the world; also some of the dullest. In some cases, these two characteristics go together. The Swiss can become wildly interested in revolutions in Venezuela, Chinese threats to Nepal, party splits in the Congo, or economic crises in Cuba, but they are not unduly agitated about goings-on in Berne. They feel a little parochial and are always shy about their own affairs; they always speak of their own politics with an apologetic smile, as a matter of no importance, i.e., of no international consequence. They seem to be a little ashamed that they never give the world any trouble, that they behave like more-or-less normal human beings and practically never threaten to plunge Europe into war, as any other small nation with a modicum of self-respect does at least twice a decade. They are fully aware that a debate over a new federal tax cannot possibly be so absorbing and exciting as a mock trial behind the Iron Curtain; and, when that new tax is abolished after a few years, that, again, is not half so dramatic as the re-

habilitation of the hanged victim when he is declared to have been after all a great patriot of shining virtue and reburied in a ceremonial grave. In other words, Swiss women would not mind having the vote in Venezuela, Nepal, the Congo, or Cuba. But in Switzerland? Oh, no, that is really not worth having.

(2) Swiss democracy has developed into something like a part-time job for men. The Swiss constitution is a federal one, like the American; each canton is, in fact, a little republic, in full control of its internal affairs, such as education, public health, police, cantonal taxes, etc. On top of it, there are federal problems and numerous municipal questions. The democratically minded Swiss have developed two special and attractive institutions—the referendum and the right of initiative. Private citizens (under conditions laid down in the constitution) are entitled to initiate legislation; the federal government can quite easily be forced to submit certain measures to referendum and, in fact, in many cases does so without any coercion at all. It is easy to see where all this overdose of democracy leads; it means that Swiss men are kept pretty busy rushing to the ballot boxes all the time. They have to voice their opinions (via the ballot box) on federal, cantonal, and municipal laws, policies, and enactments, without respite. The women, so it seems, are clever enough to stay out of this. They have enough work as it is. It is simply a happy division of labor; the women have their door knobs, the men, their ballot boxes. Two equally tedious jobs, but one has one's boring duties to perform. The women do not clamor for the vote any more than the men would be inclined to clamor for a share in polishing the door knobs.

(3) Finally, to a small extent, it is sheer heroic nasty-mindedness on the part of the men—nasty-mindedness because they take pleasure in depriving women of their natural rights. But it is also heroic, because who, I ask you, who has the courage to stand up to women? Look at America, where women are on a pedestal, simply because they put themselves on a pedestal and show little inclination to descend. Or look at Britain, where women are, I believe, the most emancipated in the world and where they gained their rights by sweat, blood,

and tears. Or look at the Communist countries, where women, having gained some genuine rights on the one hand are, on the other hand, duped by apparent concessions; now they, too, have the "right" to work in mines, to do heavy physical labor, and to slave just as a considerable section of their menfolk slave. The Swiss alone dare to carry on this eternal war of the sexes. This is the one war in which they are not neutral. They hold out, and they defy their women. The women have to do as they are told, and that's that.

But is it? No, it isn't. Swiss men are not really fooling their women; they are fooling themselves. The women do not have the vote because they do not want the vote. If they wanted it, they would have it; make no mistake about it. Thus Switzerland remains half a democracy; one half the population has no vote at all. But this disenfranchised half, if they are interested in the issue at all, tells the other half how to vote. The women still have the say; the men simply go through the motions.

MILITARISM

The Swiss, contrary to general belief, are one of the most militaristic nations of Europe. In the United States and even in the Soviet Union, a smaller and smaller percentage of the population has to serve in the armed forces. In Switzerland, there is no question of a percentage; in Switzerland, everybody is a soldier. In September, 1939, all the Swiss passes were fully manned even before Britain declared war on Germany, and today there is no country in Europe where one sees so many soldiers practicing sharpshooting, mountain climbing, or engaged in other military exercises as in Switzerland. If a nation wants to fight, it need not be very powerful; it is enough to have powerful allies. But, if you are determined to stay out of it all and not to fight, then you must be really strong.

All Swiss men are in the reserve and have to keep their uniform, full field pack, and their guns at home, ready for any

emergency. When the Swiss *Hausfrau* has finished polishing the door knobs, she gets out her husband's gun and gives it a good polish, too. There are innumerable jokes about these guns in the larder, but the point surely is that a government must trust its citizens if it can afford to keep them armed all the time. Can anyone imagine what would happen if all the citizens in, say, Hungary were given guns? A few years ago, we saw what happened even without such liberal policies. But this consideration is, of course, the most amusing of all. An outbreak of revolution in Switzerland is about as likely as an outbreak of democracy in Russia or a heat-wave in Greenland. Once a soldier, always a soldier. They simply will not let you go. There are various types of services you have to perform according to your age. People over ninety are put on slightly lighter duties—that is all.

ON MONEY

Many people say that they do not like the Swiss because they love money too much. Money has certainly become very popular with many people lately—and not only the Swiss.

The last decade has been the classical era of the businessman; money took the center of the stage, and even sex and crime were forced to play second and third fiddle. I do not think that the attitude of the Swiss toward money has lately changed much. They have always loved it, but they do not love it now any more than before. Then, it is always a question of what sort of money you love. The Swiss franc is a kind worth loving; I love it, too. It is extremely lovable.

But do the Swiss really love money? I do not think so. It is true to say that they revere it. They have a high respect for it.

To throw money around with careless, grand-seigneurish abandon is certainly not one of the conspicuous Swiss characteristics. A few years ago, I wrote a short story about a Hungarian baron who squandered two fortunes on smashing mirrors, tables, chairs, and other furniture in pubs. It was his idea of a good time. I do not say that his was a particularly intelligent or commendable pastime, but it was nothing special in prewar Hungary; it was not even remarkable. But any Swiss man worthy of his nationality would much rather die than smash one single glass deliberately, if he were to pay for it afterward.

There are few Swiss millionaires; but there are even fewer Swiss paupers. The wealth of the Swiss is solid, traditional, and inherited, even if they themselves add their mite to the family fortune. You can meet some of those rare Swiss millionaires traveling third class, because "third is just as good as first"; and in Berne you can find the president of the Swiss republic in the streetcar line, going to his office at a quarter to eight so as not to be late.

I have a Swiss friend whom I always regarded as rather un-Swiss: he is broad-minded, cosmopolitan, and very easygoing, indeed generous, with his money. I have stayed in his home on several occasions, and his hospitality was not only warm—as is usual in Switzerland—but lavish. So I was really astonished to find, when he came to stay with me in

England, that he was prepared to devote four or five days to the problem of buying a raincoat. He visited two dozen shops, returned to one many times, tried the same coat on twice a day—once in the morning and once in the afternoon—and then sped to other shops to see of he could not get a better coat cheaper. When at home, at our place, he spent half his time switching off lights in rooms where we had carelessly left them on. I decided in the end that all Swiss were alike after all and that there were no exceptions. So I was really surprised a year later when I visited him once again in Switzerland and found out something extraordinary about him. We took the funicular in his village. There were three of us—my wife, my friend, and I—but he bought only two tickets. I said nothing, but, noticing that I was somewhat perplexed, he explained, "I don't need a ticket."

"Why not?"

"I just don't," he replied somewhat curtly and mysteriously.

In the evening, he explained. His village had had no funicular, and this had offended his local pride. Why should his village be a miserable exception? It had to have a funicular, so he had one built at his own expense, which he presented to the municipality. His only condition was that he and his family were to be allowed to use it without payment to the end of time.

"Well, you deserve that much honor at least. . . ."

"Honor? Who wants honor?" he retorted. "I want to save on the fare."

Still, I did not find this explanation quite satisfactory, and I returned to the attack the next day. I asked him quite openly how could a man, capable of such generosity toward his village, be as petty as he was about a raincoat?

"You don't understand," he said. "I wanted my village to have a funicular, and a funicular costs money. Heaps of money—so I had to pay heaps. But to buy a poor raincoat when you can get a better one is waste. And waste is just stupid. For example, to illuminate your apartment as though it were a carnival is a reasonable luxury; if you like strong lights, do so by all means. But to leave lights on in an unoccupied room is waste. It is sin."

Years later, I met him by chance in a restaurant in Zürich. He asked me to sit down at his table. He was having some *antipasto* which he invited me to sample. When I declined, he insisted. Finally, I gave in, and, indeed, I had never tasted anything quite so good. So I went on tasting it. During our subsequent conversation, he told me that he had had a museum built in his village, too, and endowed it with several famous paintings.

"It must have cost as much as the funicular," I remarked.

"More," he replied drily, then asked for the bill and left.

When I rose to leave later, I noticed that the price of half an *antipasto* had been put on my bill. Well, I had tasted it.

This surprised me a little. But it should not have. And I shall certainly remember the Swiss film magnate who took me to a coffee house to discuss some business involving tens of thousands of francs and then paid for his own coffee and let me pay for mine. The idea was that the tens of thousands were to be fees, fully deserved by me; but why should he *give me*—just like that—forty centimes?

But the Gold Medal for Pettiness goes to another Swiss. Last year, I met an English girl—an old acquaintance of mine from London—in Geneva, who told me in tears that she had been defrauded by a Swiss gentleman. This sounded unlikely. And, indeed, the next day the Swiss man in question alleged that in fact it was she who had tried to cheat *him*. It turned out that this English girl had settled in Geneva and was earning her living as a translator. Translation is paid per thousand words. As a newcomer to Switzerland, she did what she had always done in England—she *estimated* the number of words and made it out to the nearest thousand.

"She charged me for 8,000 words," the outraged Swiss complained, "instead of 7,839; that is to say, 200 francs, instead of 197 francs, 15 centimes."

"But how do you know it was 7,839 words?" I asked incredulously. "You don't mean to say that you counted them? Every word?"

"Of course I counted them. And my secretary verified it. It was 7,839 all right."

I took the work home and counted the words myself. There were, in fact, 7,887 words—forty-eight more than he and his secretary had made it. I told him about this when we met the next morning. But he was even more outraged than before.

"Oh, no," he exclaimed. "Surely not. There were forty-eight *proper-nouns* in the text. You do not expect me to pay hard cash for the alleged translation of names of people or towns?"

"I certainly do," I replied. "In some cases, these names are different. Horatius is Horace in English; Vergilius is Virgil; München is Munich; and Wien is Vienna. These words surely ought to count. They have to be translated."

He was upset, because he did not want to be unfair. Mean, yes; unfair, no. It took him a whole day to work out a compromise. In the future, he said the next day, he would pay half-rate for all truly translated proper nouns (for "Wien," but not for "London"), that is, roughly one and a quarter centimes instead of two and a half.

I faithfully communicated this compromise to the translator. She listened carefully and reflected for some three or four minutes. Then she packed her bag and returned to live in England.

MERCI VIELMALS

However deep your affection for the Swiss, neither charity nor bias can go so far as to persuade you that their language —*Schwitzerdutsch*—is melodious or soothing to the ear. Its guttural noises recall Dutch; its distorted German reminds you of broken Yiddish; and the general effect reminds you of gargling during a bad attack of tonsillitis. Whenever you meet a ravishing Swiss girl—and there are plenty of them around—you gasp with admiration; but, as soon as she opens her mouth and those regurgitative noises commence, you feel like fleeing in horror. It is as though the Venus de Milo were to belch suddenly in public; one just cannot imagine the Mona Lisa speaking *Schwitzerdutsch.*

It is not only the German language that is being crucified and tormented in Switzerland. The Swiss version of French, as spoken and written in Bern officialese, is a special language of its own, usually referred to as *français fédéral.*

Then the mixed areas go a step further and germanize Gallic words, expressions, and phrases, and vice versa. You travel through a great number of villages ending with *wil,* which is, of course, the germanized version of *ville.* Or they simply let the two languages mix in the most staggering way; the expression *merci vielmals* being a fair example of this unnatural progeny. The three federal languages raise a great many problems, too. For instance—to mention only one of these—Switzerland is compelled to maintain a television service in Italian for 7,000 viewers, when 700,000 would scarcely be an adequate figure. But it is out of the question for Switzerland to have television in German, but not in French or Italian.

Whatever the Swiss may do with the federal languages—and they do quite a lot to them (and to one aspect of this language problem we shall return later)—*Schwitzerdutsch* is the real national language of Switzerland.

At first I cherished some misplaced admiration for the intelligence and common sense of the Swiss in these matters. Speaking in *Schwitzerdutsch* but writing in *Hochdeutsch* (proper German, in the Queen's German, so to speak) seemed an excellent compromise between having a language of one's own and not having it, all at the same time. The Dutch, a small nation with its own language—very similar to *Plattdeutsch* or Northwestern German—may be satisfying their national pride, but this lands them with a lot of problems; their national language brings them all the troubles of linguistic isolation, yet it is hardly more than a German dialect. The Swiss—I thought—speak their own language but write German; in other words, they have isolation when they want it, but they communicate in one of the great languages of the world when they want *that.*

Later I understood that my whole conception was based on a mistake. *Schwitzerdutsch* is not really a language; it is simply a conspiracy.

This became clear to me when I was staying with a friend near Altdorf who told me of an isolated hotel beautifully situated up in the mountains where one could spend a few days in real solitude. It was a place, I was assured, where the Swiss themselves went for their holidays. Normally, I do not seek such places; I do not want to go off the beaten track. I want the beaten track and want people around me, the more and the noisier the better. But, for one reason or another —I think I wanted to finish writing something—I decided to spend a few days in this hotel, so I called to book a room. I was told, politely but firmly, that there were no rooms. When I mentioned this to my friend, he smiled.

"Did you speak German to them?" he asked.

"Of course," I replied. "I cannot expect them to speak English."

"They speak better English than you do," said my friend, "but that's not the point."

He phoned again, spoke in *Schwitzerdutsch,* explained that I, though a foreigner, was a friend of his and booked a room for me. I found the hotel practically empty. But, if you try to book a room in German, it is always full up.

Still later, when I got to know Switzerland better, I realized that *Schwitzerdutsch* is not simply a conspiracy against the foreigner only; it is a conspiracy against the Swiss, too.

A Swiss friend of mine married a charming American girl and took her to live in his home town of Schwyz. The girl—I shall call her Susie here—accomplished the rare feat of learning *Schwitzerdutsch* without a trace of an accent. Her achievement was the more admirable in that she did not speak one word of German.

"I don't want to be regarded as a foreigner in my husband's country—well, in my own country, that is," she explained.

A few years later, they moved to Zürich, a few miles away. I went to visit them, and one day I went shopping with her. To my greatest astonishment, she spoke nothing but English to all the pushcart men and street traders or used sign language. Driving home, I asked her, "What happened? Have you forgotten your Schwitzerdutsch?"

She did not answer for a long time. Then she said bitterly, "There is no such language as *Schwitzerdutsch*. I thought there was, but the joke was on me, I guess. There is *Zürcherdutsch;* there is *Baslerdutsch;* there is *Schwyzerdutsch;* and there is *St. Gallendutsch*. And five dozen other dutsch's. When I started to use the language I learned in Schwyz, all these good people started nudging each other with their elbows or exchanging knowing looks. I wasn't speaking *Zürcherdutsch*. I was a wretched foreigner. Almost an enemy. I am better off with English. . . ."

ON INVASION AND THE FREEDOM TO DETEST ONE ANOTHER

Switzerland suffered no foreign invasion between the time of Napoleon and the middle 1950's. The Napoleonic invasion was given short shrift; the help of its allies coupled with the staunch resistance of the Swiss dealt with that threat. But that was an easy problem. Napoleon and his army tried to conquer the Swiss with only guns and swords; the new invaders, the German businessmen, use money. And the Swiss have always found it much easier to resist bullets than cash.

In the past few years, the Germans, who have always been passionately devoted to the South and the sun, invaded Ticino (the Italian-speaking canton) to such an extent that the people have become seriously worried. A great deal of the land is being bought up; modern and functional villas of exceptional ugliness are being built; German as a language is almost replacing Italian; and soon there will be standing room only in the Ticino. Watching the Gotthard Tunnel at Easter—the endless lines of German cars waiting to be taken across—one has the impression of being in Bavaria. The Germans, of course, bring money with them, spread prosperity, and there is nothing wrong with them. Nevertheless, some Swiss—mostly those not in a position to profit from the soaring price of real estate—blame the people of Ticino for selling out to the Germans. Many others, quite genuinely and without any ulterior motive, dislike the idea that the Germans, having lost the Cameroons, are now colonizing southern Switzerland instead.

There is an invasion of American businessmen, too. They prefer to have their European head offices in Switzerland, because money is freely transferable from there even to America, and the Swiss policy of neutrality also has a soothing effect on their nerves. Besides, you can always make a bargain with the tax authorities.

But the real troubles in Switzerland are always domestic, and the only invasion of consequence is also an internal one. Switzerland being a trilingual country, it would seem to be the duty of any good Swiss to pick up all three federal languages. But there is one-way traffic only. The French-speaking Swiss never learn German, and *Schwitzerdutsch* they regard as a barbaric dialect. Those of Italian mother tongue learn neither French nor German, unless, of course, they happen to get a job in a French- or German-speaking area and they have to. They are the industrious German-speaking Swiss who travel to the French parts in great numbers and learn French. Your French-Swiss friends, when you meet a waitress or a shop assistant with a heavy German accent, will sigh with disgust and exchange sad, ferocious looks: "The enemy within the walls. . . ."

The Swiss covet no territory from any other country, and no Swiss territory has secessionist ideas. Their surplus energy is also used up internally. The only secessionist movement is boiling up in the canton of Berne, which is the largest canton and is, of course, German-speaking. But it has an enclave of French-speakers who wish to secede and form a new canton, to be called Jura. This is, by the way, *merci vielmals* country, so proud of its pure Gallic tongue.) Mild and civilized demonstrations take place, subdued speeches are made, and occasionally slogans of *Jura Libre!* are painted on the walls. The rebel complex is as strong in some people as the inferiority complex or the Oedipus complex is in others; yet these poor, heroic souls have no better cause to rebel against than the vile oppression of Canton Berne.

A Bernese cantonal official told me: "We are going to suppress the movement."

"How?" I asked him with keen interest. "Are you going to open fire? Call in the troops? Is there going to be a Swiss Sharpeville?"

"Of course not. There are more subtle and much more effective methods. I shall explain to them what independent cantonal administration *costs*. I assure you, what with police, roads, schools, administrative buildings, and many other items, it comes to a pretty penny. That will cool their secessionist fever."

The internal peace, balance, and wise tolerance of the Swiss nation are based, as I have already said, on a healthy mutual detestation of one another. This is really the main clue to the wisdom of the Swiss. If "Love thy neighbor as thyself" is the first Christian duty of any true-born Swiss, "Hate thy neighbor more than thyself" is the second. Nidwalden and Obwalden are the smallest cantons (really only subcantons) in Switzerland, but the fact that Nidwalden fought against Napoleon more than a century and a half ago, whereas Obwalden did not, is still the source of undying enmity between the two races. (The races of Nidwalden and Obwalden, I mean.) A Nidwalden man once told me: "Intermarriage is quite out of the question. I would rather give my daughter to a man of Winterthur than to someone from Obwalden." "Rather to a man of Winterthur . . . !"—Believe me, these are strong words.

Or take Basle just once again. They regard themselves, and with some justification, as more French than Swiss and even more German than Swiss; after all, the Rhine is their river. People from Basle hop over to Alsace for supper and for a business conference to Germany; crossing the frontier means no more to them than crossing the street does to us.

"There is no prostitution in Basle," a Basler friend once told me. "Not because we are so virtuous; but, you see, we hop over to Paris much too often. . . ."

In spite of this valuable piece of information, I could not help noticing in the streets of Basle that my informant was not quite truthful, and I said so the next day. He grinned. "Oh, we must have a few girls. . . . They are for the sake of visiting Zürich businessmen. . . ."

When he noticed my somewhat astonished face, he added in haste: "I don't want you to misunderstand me. I do not hate the Zürchers. . . . I only despise them."

ON MOUNTAINS

Even the most superficial observer is bound to notice sooner or later that there are mountains in Switzerland; and mountains —as man has been aware from the earliest times—are great shapers of character. Swiss life has been a wonderful and, on the whole, successful struggle against the hardships of nature. Today, if you arrive via excellent roads at a solitary inn at an altitude of 12,000 feet and you find you cannot get the sort of cheese or brand of beer you are used to—only six other brands—you grumble; and the Swiss proprietor will cast down his eyes in shame.

It is the congestion and bustle of urban life that make you suspicious and sharp-witted. The men of the mountains trust one another and have plenty of time to think their problems over, or, to put the same idea a shade less politely, not even their greatest admirers would allege that the Swiss as a nation are particularly witty or quick on the uptake. When you go into a restaurant (in certain districts) and sit down at a table, a girl will come and ask you what you want. You tell her that you want to eat something. She has to establish this first, since people, after all, frequently go to restaurants for many reasons. Some go there to bathe; others to skate; others again to write poetry. But, as soon as you have told her that you personally have come to eat, she sees your point, and she may bring you the menu. Then, again, she may not, if she forgets.

Once, a friend of mine had a large piece of cake in a *confiserie*, which he greatly enjoyed. He asked the waitress, "Do you have any more of this cake?"

The girl replied, "Yes, we have," and walked away.

But she must have had afterthoughts about this, because about two minutes later she came back and asked my friend, "Do you want to see it?" She looked proud of herself for having fathomed the deep meaning of his inquiry.

The urban Swiss, though fully aware of this phenomenon, claim that only the Bernese are so exceptionally slow-witted, and, indeed, there are innumerable jokes about the slow-mindedness of the Bernese. The following quip is often repeated.

"What is this?" (they ask you). "Bum . . . [a minute pause], bum . . . [a minute pause], bum . . . [a minute pause], bum. . . ."

If you haven't already guessed, it is a Bernese machine gun.

The Bernese themselves laugh at these jokes good-heartedly, repeat them (missing the point here and there), and shrug their shoulders.

"We are slow-witted," the above-quoted Bernese official told me, "because we are mountain peasants and not New York gossip columnists. The valleys limit one's horizons. We don't see too far. And our slow-wittedness is, of course, a piece of great good luck for Switzerland. Do you think that it is simply coincidence that Berne is the capital of Switzerland? Of course not. We are not excitable, we do not hurry into things, we ponder over matters, and the eternity of the mountain tops governs all our decisions. If Switzerland were ruled by the foxy traders of Zürich or the wits of Basle, we would have ten times as many troubles, quarrels, and disputes with others as we have now."

Mountain people are not too chatty, not too communicative, and always stand on their dignity. In some mountain villages, funerals are the main festive occasions. Part of the funeral ceremony is a collection; everybody has to throw a ten-centime piece into the box and may take in exchange a ten-centime cigar. Some of the aged poor cannot afford this money for cigars. In other communities in other lands, they would probably be given the cigars free. But charity is the ugliest of all virtues, and it is so humiliating. So these old people are allowed to throw an old button into the collection box, and they get real cigars in exchange. Everyone knows that they are buttons they put in, and they know that everyone knows. Yet, the ritual survives because the concept of human dignity survives. Real dignity based on a sham—can anything be kinder, more human than that?

Switzerland is (with the exception of Britain) perhaps the last remaining country in the world where quality is still valued and good craftsmanship appreciated. Ours is the civilization of the assembly line, the cheap department store, and vulgar mass production; and I am an enthusiastic supporter of this in all its forms. I revere the firm of Marks and Spencer in England, which made it possible for every shop girl and factory worker to dress and look like a duchess; marksandspencerism has done more for the equality of the human race than has Marxism. Nevertheless, pride in one's work, in craftsmanship, the appreciation of something good simply because it *is* good and beautifully made is another virtue which is, alas, slowly dying out—but not in Switzerland. That does not mean, however, that the Swiss are old-fashioned. Oh, no! If you have ever attempted to climb a mountain, you know that new panoramas and vistas open before you every minute. The mountaineer's horizon may be limited in the valleys; but his view is a constantly varying one, and he is used to novelty and change. Indeed, the otherwise-conservative and old-fashioned Swiss love everything new, simply for the sake of novelty. They will try everything once; there is no country which is farther from America, in some respects, and no country is nearer, in others. When I was in Switzerland recently we read in the newspapers that the first electric computer was being installed in Holland, another small and rich Western European country. The Swiss could hardly believe this. They had at least a hundred computers already; even medium-sized firms had bought them, just for the hell of it, just to see what these things are really like. Packing is a major art in Switzerland, and the amount of new ideas and charm that go into making up parcels never fails to stagger English visitors. One could say about quite a few matters: what Basle is doing today, London will be doing tomorrow. But London is not so quick in learning. What Basle is doing today, London will be doing, perhaps, next week or next month—with cautious and suspicious restraint. I stayed in a new hotel in Basle; everything was pushbutton and the last word in modernity. There were red, green, and yellow lights indicating and sometimes fulfilling all your possible and impossible desires. You had your private safe in each room, and you could have your private airplane chartered by the hotel if you wished. I did not happen so to wish, but I thought nostalgically of English country hotels where the procedure is as follows: if you want something, you push the button marked "chambermaid," wait five minutes, and then get it yourself.

And, finally, the men of the mountains are tough and rugged, too. I do not say that every Swiss traveling salesman is a William Tell. But the amount of work; endurance; courage; and sheer, mulish stubbornness that must have gone into turning rugged and rocky Switzerland into the modern Paradise it is must make the pyramids of Egypt blush. There is a Swiss joke about the toughness of the Nidwalden people, and it is, in a way, characteristic of the whole nation. A Nidwalden soldier who was taking part in some old-fashioned military exercises was hit by an arrow which pinned him to a tree, so that he could not free himself or even move for nine hours. At last he was found by a comrade of his (a Zürcher merchant), who asked him with sympathy, "Does it hurt?" The man replied, "Only when I laugh."

HOW TO AVOID WINTER SPORTS

Whenever I go to Switzerland in the winter, my chief problem is how to avoid winter sports. It is not an easy task. Dangers lurk in every corner. In November or so, the whole country is transformed into one vast—well, not so terribly vast—ski run, and few of your kind and hospitable Swiss friends seem able to grasp that your main purpose in life is not to run down a mountain slope at fifty miles an hour as if you were a sixty-horsepower automobile with faulty brakes.

The railways cease to carry any goods other than skis; and the countryside is transformed into a white infinity, broken only by ski lifts carrying small, blue figures and their strange equipment. Whoever is not actually skiing has just finished skiing or is just about to go out skiing—and that applies to the ski-lift operator, the railway conductor, the waiter in your hotel, and also to that elderly chambermaid who you thought could hardly walk. You were right; she can hardly walk, but she can ski. Those few people who are not skiing are busy skating, tobogganing, mountaineering, curling, or are out on a run of skijoring.

If I am so keen to avoid winter sports, the reader might—not unreasonably—ask: Why do I go to Switzerland in winter? The answer is that I usually have some other business to attend to; second, I love Switzerland in the winter, just as in any other season; third, I am addicted to my own, private winter sport, that is, to avoid skiing. Believe me, it needs much more determination and skill not to ski in Switzerland than to ski.

My aversion to skiing is purely personal. I am not too much of a duffer in sports that depend largely on one's hands (such as tennis, golf, boxing, or, preferably, darts, table tennis or billiards), but I am utterly and ridiculously hopeless in all sports in which you have to rely on your feet. Since my earliest youth, I have been at war with my feet, and my feet have always won. They have defeated me regularly. For eleven years, I went skating; one day my younger brother joined me and I was deeply moved to see that, after one afternoon's practice, he was a much better skater than I was after eleven years. That was the end of my career on ice.

Or, rather, the end of it, with the exception of curling. Curling is a game the Swiss play in a breather between a giant slalom and a round on skates or whenever they can spare a little time between tobogganing and skijoring. The game consists of pushing two metal hot-water bottles around on the ice—a pastime which rather suits my skill and temperament. Further than that, I am not prepared to go.

Since being unable to do something myself has never deterred me from giving advice and instruction to others, I shall now tell you what you are to do if you are still determined to ski:

(1) First of all, you must join a ski school. If you are a beginner, the teacher will convince you in the first lessons that, however long you live, never in your life will you be able to learn how to ski. If you are a more advanced pupil, the first lessons will recall and confirm these early impressions. You will be ordered to make clumsy and undignified motions which you could perform with ease and grace if your skis were not in your way; yet you are not allowed to take them off. Further, whenever you look around, you will meet maliciously amused eyes of people like me, who watch from the windows of a comfortable hotel lounge or a well-heated car and derive great entertainment from your sufferings. Do not be put off by all this. In a few days, you will be surprised to see that you have made great progress and are ready for further suffering and vicissitudes.

There are, as a rule, six people in the skiing class, and all the skiing teachers keep reassuring you that fees are miserably, even shamefully low. I have yet to meet a pupil who was really ashamed to pay his fees because he found them too low, but I believe that they are certainly not ruinous.

(2) Every day you must do some shopping. Since most people prefer, at the bottom of their hearts, shopping to skiing, this part of the holiday is not regarded as a hardship by anyone. I have never met a skier who had all he (or, even more often, she) needed and who did not dash out to buy various items at least twice a day. One needs different boots, another pullover, thinner or thicker gloves, a windproof jacket, a pair of ear muffs, or at least—if one cannot think of anything better and more expensive—a pair of new sunglasses. All this, of course, besides the purchase of watches, chocolate, souvenirs, cameras, precision instruments, and so on.

(3) After a few days, when the beginner can already move, you must decide what sort of skiing you want to do. You will probably take a train, a streetcar, a funicular, or a ski lift to reach one peak or another. You may reach the first peak by bus (two francs), the second by funicular (three francs), the third by a cog-wheeled railway (four francs), the fourth by ski lift (five francs), and the fifth by cable-car (six francs). Sometimes there is a sixth peak, too; they shoot you up there by cannon at the modest price of seven francs. (Half the fare returnable if you do not arrive in one piece.) Most people seem to dote on

these journeys. I have seen quite a number of them who make eight or nine such journeys a day; as soon as they reach the bottom of a run on skis, they start off up again. They carry timetables in their pockets and work out complicated connections between cog-railway and ski lift, so as to outdo the man who sits next to them at dinner.

(4) Take singing and yodeling lessons without delay. In the evenings, the whole country, natives and visitors alike, bursts out in song and yodeling. I have not found out why skiing is so conducive to singing, but yodeling and howling seem to be at least as popular a winter sport as skiing. I do not indulge in either, but admit that each has its points. Skiing is much less noisy; singing, on the other hand, is much less dangerous.

(5) The dangers, however, should not be overestimated. Before writing this, I met in my club a Swiss friend, a passionate skier, whose brother is a doctor, and I asked him to tell me something about the dangers of skiing. "It is nonsense to call skiing dangerous," he said. "Only an infinitesimal proportion of people come to grief, and the great majority have no trouble whatever. Nevertheless," he added thoughtfully, "Swiss doctors are apt to complain. They are always busier in the winter than they like to be, and that, unfortunately, interferes with their own skiing."

(6) If you are really good, soon nothing will be steep, long, and fast enough for you. You will find the 3,300 feet of Engelberg ridiculous, the 6,000 feet of the Jochpass not quite up to your standards, St. Moritz not steep enough for your liking, the ten miles from Davos to Küblis too short, and even the run from Gornergrat to Zermatt—a five-and-a-half-mile descent in about eight minutes—a trifle slow. You need not despair. There is always skijoring, a sport which has taken enormous strides in the past decade. In olden days, not-too-ferocious Swiss horses pulled people on skis across the ice at Arosa and St. Moritz. Then the American GI's arrived on the scene after the war and motorized this sport in no time by using jeeps and trucks. Even this, however, was soon found too dull. So nowadays they are

experimenting with ordinary airplanes; the plane runs on the ice, and you hang on behind. Should it take off, do not forget to let go of the ropes. Even the tougher kind of sportsman finds it a little irksome crossing Switzerland hanging from a plane. But, even if the plane does not take off, a word of warning is found necessary in connection with this new craze. A Swiss guidebook I have before me soberly remarks about skijoring-cum-airplanes: "The average tourist may not have the necessary skill to participate in this sport." I wonder. I have never met an average tourist—at least not in Switzerland and after a week's skiing—who admitted that he lacked the skill for anything under the sun.

If you are looking for even tougher assignments, the only thing you can do is join the Swiss army. In the course of their training, Swiss soldiers race over the middle part of *La Haute Route*. It takes twenty-four hours nonstop, and I have yet to meet the skiing enthusiast who would not find that run tough enough.

ON FOOD

I am no drunkard, but I love Swiss soups. No one who has tasted a variety of Swiss soups will be astonished by this statement, because he will know that the Swiss love to put *Kirsch*—a kind of cherry brandy—in everything they eat, particularly their soups. Many good people get roaring drunk on Swiss soups before they know what has hit them. And, in a popular Swiss winter resort, I once saw a patriotic Englishman get to his feet, raise his soup plate, and call out in a loud voice, "Ladies and Gentlemen: the Queen."

In Switzerland, many of the girls are as beautiful and many of the men as lanky, sporty types as are to be seen anywhere in the world; but you can see as many fat people, too, as in the most sedentary countries of Europe. Quite a few Swiss are worried about their obesity and devote much ingenuity to finding reasons for it. They will give you many scientific answers, but only few hit on the very unscientific explanation—because they eat too much. A slice of apple tart in Switzerland is a foot around, a portion of cheese reminds you of the cheese counter in the average English grocer's, and they eat piles of whipped cream. They are always darting off to their excellent *confiseries* on the slightest provocation, and their purpose is not to abstain from sweet, sugary, and creamy things. A worried Swiss lady once told me, "I don't know why I am still gaining weight. . . . Honestly, I eat only half the amount of whipped cream I used to. . . ."

Swiss restaurants, too, make universal use of a shrewd trick to entice you into an early grave through overfeeding. They have a cunning habit of serving only *half* your portion at a time. You fail to notice this because half a portion in Switzerland looks like a whole portion anywhere else. So you eat your share—with some difficulty because even half is more than enough—and then along comes the waitress, all smiles, and dishes out the other half. If you are as weak a character as I am, you eat that, too.

Swiss food is, on the whole, good and healthy, but, I think, the Swiss cuisine cannot compete with the finesse of the French. I am, however, one of the greatest living connoisseurs of sausages, which I regard as one of the supreme creations of the human race. Now, the Austrians and the Bavarians are no mean sausage nations by any standards, but the Swiss excel them all, by virtue of a giant sausage called the *Schüblig*. What Shakespeare is among writers, the *Schüblig* is among sausages. A nation which gave the *Schüblig* to undeserving humanity is a nation of giants and must be forgiven anything, including its winter sports and including its impudence in being a tiny people which yet sets a shining example to the whole world on how to behave normally; how to live graciously; how to act sensibly in a mad world; how to hate your friends and neighbors; and how to be able to love humanity—which, if you come to think of it, deserves neither their love nor their *Schüblig*.

6

BRITAIN
FRANCE
ITALY
GERMANY
SWITZERLAND
√ ISRAEL
JAPAN

ARRIVAL

At Cyprus airport, the three Greek Orthodox priests and one or two others got out; when, an hour later, we took off for Lydda, I found the atmosphere of the plane completely changed. All the customary reserve and shyness of the travelers were gone. "The next stop is the right one," exclaimed joyfully a middle-aged, Blimpish-looking gentleman who had not uttered one word between London and Cyprus. People were walking up and down the plane, everybody was talking to everybody else, all using words I did not quite understand, and "next Wednesday" suddenly became "after Rosh Hashana." My neighbor, a young man with a red RAF moustache, grasped my hand: "I am a carpenter from Glasgow."

"Oh," I replied, after some hesitation, nothing wittier having occurred to me.

"I've given up everything," he went on. "Sold my house and

workshop. My wife and child will follow me soon. I want to live here."

"Why did you leave? Anti-Semitism?"

He threw an astonished glance at me.

"No. Not at all. People were very decent over there. But I've told you. I just want to live here."

A few minutes later, he turned to me again:

"Look. There's land over there. What is it?"

I looked at the little map I had picked up in the plane and told him that it was the shores of Israel. All the passengers crowded on our side and looked out. Then the carpenter from Glasgow started singing the Jewish national anthem softly in a very self-conscious voice. Almost all the others joined in, including the two fat American ladies who, up to now, had tried to behave like detached foreign tourists who might have gone to Bermuda or Hawaii, but, as it happened, had picked Israel by chance.

We landed, and a very good-looking girl in a gray uniform entered the plane. She declared, first in Hebrew, then in English: "Ladies and gentlemen, you are welcome in Israel. Please, follow me."

The carpenter from Glasgow, unable to control himself any longer, threw himself at the girl and kissed her. I took a very poor view of his action, but later, when I saw him kiss the customs official, too, I realized that his fervor had been purely patriotic. It takes a great deal of unselfish patriotism to make one kiss a customs official.

WHEN A JEW BECOMES AN ISRAELI

The West, Central, and East European has a general picture of the Jews which is about as accurate as the observation that all cats are shrewd or that, all Englishmen are tall, silent, and never stop smoking pipes. They believe that the Jews are clever merchants, but in Tel Aviv shops the Israeli shopkeepers do not press you to buy. If you stop in front of a shop window, you may

stand there till the end of your life and they will not try to lure you in, in sharp contrast to the rest of the Middle Eastern (and many other) countries. The Jews have the reputation of being very clever in money matters, too, but the new state is almost as broke as it would be if it were an ancient and famous world power and empire. The Jews have the reputation (mostly in Central and Eastern Europe, where anti-Semitic propaganda sank in deeper than in Britain) of being indifferent soldiers; but the young and practically untrained Israeli army beat the armies of five Arab states. (It is true that the Arabs fought badly; this does not alter the fact that the Israelis fought well.) The Jews have the reputation (even in Britain, where in this respect anti-Semitic propaganda *was* successful) of being excellent black marketeers and master currency-smugglers. But there is hardly any black market in Israel, and in the worst case you can get a miserable white-market meal at black-market prices. And no Israeli victims or customers of any great international currency-juggler have been traced as yet.

The real difference between Jews and Israelis is not that the former are short, fat, dark-skinned, and hook-nosed, whereas the others are tall, thin, blond, and blue-eyed. (I shall have more to say on this subject.) Nor is the real difference that the Jews are afraid of possible new pogroms, whereas the Israelis feel safe. In many countries, the idea of a pogrom never even enters the Jews' heads, whereas many Israelis are not satisfied with their own security. The real difference is that a black marketeer in Israel is not "that Jew Katz"; he is simply called Katz or whatever his name may be and will be punished if he is found out to be a black marketeer. The same thing is true in other spheres. They do not have to emphasize what they have done for their country, because it goes without saying that they have done everything. They do not have to quote statistics to the effect that, during the war, 53, 72, or 80 per cent of the fallen soldiers were Jews. One hundred per cent were Jews, and, although they fell as Jews, they are only remembered as fallen soldiers. They do not need to keep explaining that Ehrlich and Einstein, Mendelssohn and Jascha Heifetz were or are Jews. They do not have to justify or excuse their existence with their usefulness to the community at large. They have the full right to be mediocre and insignificant—a most important and valuable freedom in a modern state.

If anyone believes that the Jews are generally disliked except in Israel, where they all love each other fondly, he is badly mistaken. I would even go as far as to state that there is a Jewish Israel and an Israeli Israel. A lady who had come from Kaunas told me in Tel Aviv: "You know, in Lithuania I was a Jew; here in Israel, I have become a Lithuanian. And, when I am among the really orthodox, I feel like a *shikse*." (*Shikse* is a derogatory word for a Christian woman.)

ISRAELI ISRAEL

If you want to get on with the Israelis, praise them. It is silly to praise people behind their backs. Not very manly either. Tell

them openly, to their faces, that you think they are wonderful. Have the courage to insist that they are admirable, brave, brilliant, efficient, noble, and inimitable. At first, I thought such statements might embarrass them. But not at all. They do not mind them. They can face the truth. They say it themselves.

•

Do not temper your praise with qualifications. Forget about such words and phrases as: ". . . although" or: "Though I appreciate . . ." or "nevertheless." They do not believe that something can be "very bad, although quite good," or "rotten, nevertheless enchanting." This is a decadent British notion. They prefer plain speaking. In Israel, everything is either very good or excellent.

Do not be afraid of singing the praise of anything. You cannot overdo it. If you visit a faculty of the university, go into every lecture room and keep on exclaiming in surprise and admiration: "How lovely! How unlike anything else I have seen, except perhaps lecture rooms all over the world!" If you go to a scientific institution, admire every single laboratory, microscope, and test tube, and, if you visit a library, be careful not to overlook a single book, or you will be accused of being an enemy of the Jewish people. They are proud of everything, even of the ruins of the recent war. "Our own ruins," they say. "Look at the destruction," they exclaim proudly.

•

No criticism is taken in good humor. If something is absolutely and quite obviously indefensible, they will tell you that it is an inheritance from the Mandate and that they have had no time as yet to put it right.

Every single Israeli is a propagandist, and usually a bad one. They keep telling you in Mograbi, Tel Aviv's Piccadilly Circus: "Fifty years ago, this place was a desert." Or, in a park: "Three years ago, this place was a wilderness." Often they go back as far as two thousand years. The opening of the first Israeli railway, the Tel Aviv–Haifa line, was almost a national holiday. I heard from at least thirty people that it was two thousand years since a Jew last drove an engine of the Jewish State Railways. No doubt, their achievements are truly magnificent. Admiration for their achievements, however, is almost canceled out by the irritation caused by this permanent boasting. Just when you are about to remark, "How admirable," they pat themselves on the shoulder and say it themselves. However generous you may be, you just cannot force yourself to say more than: "Well, it's not bad."

Let's be fair. Their swaggering is irritating. And let's be still fairer: if we were in their shoes, we would boast in exactly the same way.

•

Do not forget that Israel is the center of the world. The great events are the events of the Middle East, and the world powers and their struggle are only used as pawns in the foreign policy of Israel. The great powers only provide the fence for the Israeli diplomats to sit on. The defeat of a revolution in the Balkans, mobilization against a former Cominform state, or the conquest of a continent are events of secondary importance. But, if the Israeli representative makes a five-minute speech in the subcommittee of the General Deadlock Commission of the

United Nations dealing with the development of the pottery industry in the Manaluka Islands, that is front-page news.

You may ask, What has happened to the famous Jewish sense of humor? It has certainly been lost in transit to Israel. The ability to laugh at oneself has been proclaimed by the English to be the highest expression of humor. It is not utterly impossible that the reason for this view is the fact that the English are certainly able to laugh at themselves, provided that the jokes against them are worded to the effect that even they, such admirable and nearly perfect fellows, have tiny little faults (no, I would not call them faults—weaknesses), such as being foolishly goodhearted, exaggeratedly noble, and too much aware of their own superiority over all past, present, and future peoples of the Earth, Mars, Uranus, and Neptune. The Jews used to have this characteristic in common with the English, though their irony at their own expense was much more cruel and realistic. Why the English and the Jews? First, because irony at one's own expense is a trait of old and wise peoples. (Now the old Jewish race has been rejuvenated into the young Israeli nation.) Second, because irony at one's own expense is one of the fortunate by-products of the ghetto spirit. The ghetto is an island, and splendid isolation only creates a ghetto in the global sense.

The Israelis take themselves very seriously. They cannot laugh at anybody or anything. It is not the tragedy of the recent past which has blunted and foiled their sense of humor; it is the successes and the achievements of the present. If they build a house, it is too magnificent for words, and they see nothing funny in it. Indeed, there is nothing funny in a house, except that they admire it with such reverence.

•

There are also, however, some gains to be recorded. A group of young Israeli children in a *kibbutz* were shown a documentary film on concentration camps. They sat through the performance, and at the end all declared that the whole thing was completely untrue. People argued with them; the children were told that the films had been based on facts and the scenes reconstructed by people who knew. They shrugged their shoulders and said the whole thing was propaganda. An American journalist friend and I drew two children aside, two boys of about fourteen, and asked them what their reasons were for this peculiar conclusion.

"It's too silly for words," replied one of them. "It just can't possibly be true. These people were treated like dogs and worse. They were beaten up. And yet they did not fight back."

The young Israeli may have forgotten how to laugh. But he has learned to hit back. At the moment, it is, all things considered, a clear gain.

•

The Israelis are among the very few peoples of the world who look confidently and defiantly to the future. I found this optimistic spirit of the country more impressive than anything else. In Britain, people, consciously or unconsciously, brood over the glories of the last century. In Belgium and Hungary, in France and Greece, they keep talking of the "good old days," which means a different era for each speaker. In Vienna, they dream of the gay and happy, imperial days. In Italy, I was told by an Italian friend: "You ought to have come five hundred years ago." It is in Israel and only in Israel that people tell you: "Well, it may be wonderful. But come back in ten years." Or: "Come back in two years." Or, sometimes: "Come back next week."

MANNERS

Sometimes you meet people who fit the pattern of the old Palestine jokes. I was in a café with seven other people, and a member of our party ordered "eight teas" for us. The waiter trotted back after a few minutes with glasses of steaming, purple tea on a tray and a slice of lemon in each glass. (They serve tea and coffee in glasses, with the natural result that you

cannot touch the glass while it is hot; and, when you can touch it, it is not hot enough to drink.) The waiter put the tray down, leaving the task of distributing the glasses to us. We did so, and found one glass too many. My host called the waiter back and said to him:

"Look, we ordered eight glasses of tea, and you brought us nine."

The waiter was unimpressed. "*Nu*," he replied, "what about it? Another Yid will come and drink it."

The other Yid duly arrived and drank it.

I heard of another waiter in Nahariya (a holiday resort north of Acre) who had been somewhat rudely reprimanded by a German customer for some minor mistake. The waiter listened patiently to a long and vociferous rigmarole which ended with these words:

"No, I'm sure you've never been a waiter in the London Ritz."

Upon which the waiter replied placidly:

"And I'm sure you've never been a guest in the London Ritz."

A gentleman I met, a dance-band leader of the same town, told me that once he had been looking for a crooner. A man—in type and appearance rather unlike Messrs. Sinatra and Crosby—stopped him in the street and applied for the job.

"What sort of voice have you?"

"Very beautiful."

"I don't mean that," he replied. "Are you a bass?"

"Sure. I'm a bass."

"That's no good, I'm afraid. I want a tenor."

"Oh, but I'm a tenor, too."

This kind of behavior, however, is rare. Israel is very much unlike a Jewish joke. People are Jewish, but they are Jewish in quite a different way. People's manners are exactly the same as in many European cities and much better than in some. I very much liked the complete absence of pomposity in offices, including the highest offices and ministries. If you are looking for Mr. Soandso—a high official, let us say, in the Foreign Ministry—the receptionist will tell you: "Room three, first floor." No telephone calls, and in nine cases out of ten no secretaries trying to look coolly efficient. You knock at his door and walk in. I did not meet one person who tried to impress me with the importance of his position. Once I was introduced to a gentleman in the hall of a Jerusalem hotel. We, about five persons altogether, had a hearty chat about England, my visit and impressions in Israel, and some new books. It was only after he left that I learned that he was a member of the government. I do not think that this could have happened anywhere else.

People are usually matter-of-fact, brief, and polite. Their politeness is not of the Central European or Balkan kind—

which is much more Oriental—nor does it resemble the verbose German courtesy; nor do they ask you to tell your life story and explain your specific reasons for inquiring where Schlesinger Street is, as some Americans would do. They tell you: "first right, second left" and walk off before you have a chance to say "thank you." Indeed, their politeness is of the English brand. Even one of the former terrorist leaders—a neat, rather shy man with a soft voice and a tendency to blush—told me once with a sigh: "The inheritance the English left does not consist entirely of bad things."

There is one habit which is clearly of British origin—that of queueing. Unlike the British, they have no passion for queueing; they do not like queueing for queueing's sake. But they stick to the queueing etiquette, form orderly queues at many places, and guard their rights with a morose kind of vigilance. Once, at a bus stop, a man wanted to jump the queue and get on the bus first. A Moroccan Jew drew his knife—they are just as quick with them as the Arabs—and cut off the offender's left ear.

Good manners clearly mattered greatly to this man.

THE HEBREW LANGUAGE

In other, normal, countries almost every citizen speaks the language of the land without a foreign accent, but there are quite a few people who cannot read and write. In Israel, only a fraction of the population speaks proper and faultless Hebrew, and, although there are in Israel fewer illiterates than in most other countries, the number of the people who can speak Hebrew is much larger than the number of those who can read and write it. In 1950, about one third of the population had arrived in the country in the previous eighteen months, which, proportionately, in Britain would mean fifteen million and, in the United States, forty-five million immigrants or refugees in a year and a half. Hebrew is, moreover, not an easy language to pick up. I used to know many Germans and Austrians in Hungary who had been living there for forty years and spoke Hungarian fluently but could never have conjugated a verb correctly and had atrocious accents. And Hebrew is more difficult than Hungarian, which is not a kind of Esperanto either. I—this may sound boastful, but I must not refrain from speaking the truth even if it is flattering to me—succeeded in picking up well over half a dozen words in a few weeks. Mine was regarded as fairly good Hebrew, so I do not hesitate to write this little etymological essay on the Hebrew language and give advice and guidance to beginners.

Hebrew is written without vowels, as though in English, let us say, the British national anthem were to be written thus:

Gd sv r nbl Qn,
Gd sv r grcs Qn,
Gd sv th Qn.

This might be understood, but it is clearly not the type of spelling reform advocated by enthusiasts. The difficulties in Hebrew are obvious and manifold, the two main ones being these:

Take the English word, "dog." If the English had adopted the Hebrew way of spelling (and, considering the kind of spelling they did adopt, it would have been but a small step further), "dog" would be written, "dg." In this sentence: "th dg ws brkng ldly" (provided you knew that the rest of the words meant, "the . . . was barking loudly), you would jump to the conclusion that "dg," in this context, stands for "dog." After all, you would naïvely ask, who would bark loudly but a dog. But "dg," in a vowelless spelling could stand for many things, for instance, "dig," "dag," "dug," "Doge," "Dago," "edge," "adage," and "adagio." In a music critic's notice, the above sentence might well be read: "the adagio was barking loudly"—as, indeed, it so often does. Wll, wll, wll. . . .

One may object that all this is unfair because I take my examples from English, and my knowledge of Hebrew is next to nothing. I could reply that since my Hebrew is next to nothing, it is equally unfair to expect me to take my examples from Hebrew. However, I collected many examples, and here I give you a not uninteresting one: *svr* in Hebrew may mean either *saver*, "hope," or *shever*, "the destruction of the spirit," i.e., exact opposites.

One might suggest that they should perfect their alphabet by inventing signs for the vowels. But this has already been done, and children's books and beginners' manuals are printed in this way. The vowels are represented by dots and dashes placed *under* the letters in various combinations. The general acceptance of this way of spelling, however, would make printing extremely difficult and setting on Linotype impossible. They ought to design letters for the Linotype machine in such a way that each consonant, in addition to its vowelless root form, should have variants for each vowel combination, for example, the series "b"—*ba, be, bi, bo, bu,* and *by* for each single letter. The alphabet would consist of about 300 letters, which would be enough to drive any printer mad.

Another difficulty besetting the Hebrew language is lack of words. There is a Hebrew Language Academy which manufactures such new words as "ball bearing" and "jet propulsion" on the assembly line. This is all to the good; in any case these words have only lately been manufactured in all the other countries. A more serious trouble is that the language got a little rusty lying around in dusty cupboards for centuries, and it is not quite up to the task of expressing the thoughts of modern intellectuals. As Arthur Koestler put it, "You can't play a scherzo on a ram's horn." Koestler's statement was seriously and angrily criticized, rejected, and condemned. People told me that he was not in a position to know, since his knowledge of Hebrew was just above the average, consequently still very poor. All the experts I pumped on the subject maintained that Hebrew was a rich and beautiful language (which no one doubts) perfectly able to express the widest range of feelings and thoughts (which many people doubt). "We translate the greatest masterpieces of world literature into Hebrew," they told me. Indeed, they work wonders, and the appearance of *Hamlet* in Hebrew was almost a national holiday. Two of my experts, however, gave themselves away under the fire of my cross-examination. They admitted that the language was all right for Shakespeare, Goethe, and Tolstoy, but a number of much lesser lights—some contemporary humorists for example—could not be translated, because the language is just not suitable for light irony and wit. It just would not come off. It seems to be, after all, the story of the scherzo and the ram's horn.

The Hebrew language was revived for everyday use by Ben Yehuda, who lived from 1858 to 1922. In his youth, he was a student at the Russian university at Dvinsk. He emigrated to Palestine and refused to talk to his wife, children, or any stranger, except in Hebrew. "I don't say a Zionist must be insane. But it helps if he is." (This is attributed to the late

Chaim Weizmann who said it—if he said it at all—some decades ago.) Indeed, the fanatic Ben Yehuda was for long considered raving mad by many. But the habit of speaking Hebrew caught on, and he achieved the impossible. The resurrection of the language is an even stranger and more remarkable phenomenon than the resurrection of the state. "To have one's own language is the root of human dignity," wrote Aristotle, and it is mainly due to this remarkable man, Ben Yehuda, that today milk men and tailors, postmen and lawyers, officials and waiters speak Hebrew. They may speak it well or indifferently, but they speak it as naturally as French or Persian is spoken.

Ben Yehuda himself derived his knowledge of Hebrew from the Bible, and that is one reason why the Bible occupies a special place in Jewish history. In the cases of other languages, a great literary work is a by-product of the language; in this case, the language is the by-product of a great literary work.

The faults of heaviness and clumsiness in this case are faults of youth—youth in a reincarnated existence, but still youth. It will be cured in time. The scherzo's day may not have come yet, but newspapers and books are written in Hebrew; it is spoken in Parliament and in the street; the Hebrew University teaches all the sciences in Hebrew and has all the necessary textbooks; and a healthy and powerful slang—school, town, and military—is developing. Today, Hebrew is already the language of the drawing room; tomorrow, it will be the language of the bedroom. And then it will have come of age.

•

There is something peculiar in Israel for the visitor or newcomer in the fact that normal and trivial life is going on at places which are associated in our minds with the sacred and mysterious birth of religions. For the visitor, Bethlehem is the place where Jesus was born; for the neighborhood, it is a bus terminus and is now a village under Arab domination. Nazareth, for you, may be the place where Mary lived at the time of the Immaculate Conception; for Paul Schweiger of Tel Aviv, it is the place where orange juice can be bought fairly cheaply. Beersheba was Abraham's country, but, if it has any importance for Moshe Klug in Safed, it is because his brother is stationed there. Similarly, one can hardly get over one's surprise that the holy letters of the scriptures are used to advertise women's underwear and movie stars' legs are emblazoned on neon advertisements. It may be silly to be surprised at all this. I am sure that it is. Still, I can well understand the English schoolteacher in a Wiltshire village who, when she asked one of her pupils, "Where were you born?" and received the answer, "In Jerusalem," was outraged and exclaimed in horror, "What sacrilege!"

MONEY

From 1938 (when I first arrived in England) until 1949, I naïvely thought that the British monetary system was the most complicated in the world. I also thought that weights and measures could not be sillier than in Britain. I know that Americans also measure weights in pounds and ounces; still, I have reduced American professors of mathematics to tears when I introduced *stones* into our conversation. They knew nothing of stones. They wanted to learn nothing of stones.

Now I have learned that the British system is comparatively reasonable. The Palestinians have committed the fatal mistake of trying to rationalize the British monetary system. It must be obvious to everybody at first glance that the British monetary system cannot stand up to the strains of rationalization. It is like an attempt to rationalize the *Bab Ballads* or Edward Lear; it is like telling a shaggy-dog story in the language of metaphysics or reciting the facts of the *Walrus and the Carpenter* in the phraseology of a King's counsel opening for the Crown. Yet, that is what the people of Palestine did. They took the pound

and sprinkled it with the decimal system. The result is a lap dog with two heads and three tails.

The Israeli pound (I£) is the successor of the Palestine pound (P£). An I£ is equivalent to a British pound sterling. So far so good. (Or *was*, until a few years ago.)

You buy a few envelopes and ask the fatal question: "How much are they?" The reply is: "One shilling." You give the shopkeeper a coin with the number 1 on it. It depends on his temperament whether he hands it back to you with a polite smile or flings it in your face. I must add that Israeli shopkeepers are rather temperamental. A shilling is in fact five piastres; consequently, you have to hand him a coin with the number . . . did you say 5? Wrong again. With the number 50.

The main thing to remember is this. When they speak of a piastre, they mean ten mills; when they speak of a shilling, they mean fifty prutoth; when an elderly gentleman says "a franc," he really means five prutoth, i.e., a coin which does not exist at all. (It is exactly like talking of a guinea.) When the same elderly gentleman says "a girsh," he means one fifth of a shilling, and, when he says, "a grusch," you are driven completely crazy.

Yet, strange as it may seem, there is a clue to all this. An I£ is divided into 1,000 prutoth. Why? Do not ask me. That is the official decision, and that should be the end of it. But the Israelis are an unofficially minded nation, and prutoth (*pruta,* in singular) are just not mentioned. A pruta used to be called a mill in the times of the Mandate. A mill is sometimes mentioned, but rarely. What they do mention often is the piastre, which, however, does not exist. If it did, it would consist of ten mills, and this supposition is the basis of the Israeli monetary system. Lest that be too simple for you, they also count in shillings, which do not exist either. If the shilling existed, it would be five piastres, which does not exist, but, if it did, five piastres would be fifty prutoth, but prutoth is never mentioned. It is obvious that even these difficulties could be mastered with willpower and perseverance. So some elderly people keep talking of "girsh," which is Arabic for "piastre" (but piastre does not exist). Yiddish-speaking people will speak of a "grusch." That is the easiest of all. "Grusch" is simple Yiddish for "girsh," which (just to refresh your memory) is Arabic for "piastre," which latter does not exist. If all this is now clear to you, the only other thing to remember is that a franc is half a grusch, i.e., five prutoth (which is never mentioned), i.e., half a girsh which does not exist.

I would advise the reader to read this section over again very carefully, then take two aspirins and go to bed.

TWO CITIES

Tel Aviv is, in normal circumstances, one hour's drive from Jerusalem. In spite of their geographical proximity, a great gulf separates the two cities. Within the small confines of Israel, you will be struck by the great variety of landscape. In the space of a few hours, you pass from the Mediterranean to the Oriental; mild, almost smiling valleys alternate with desolate, barren hills; cities of white marble, with the pale-green desert. All this variety of external appearance as well as of character is nowhere so marked as in the two main cities, Tel Aviv and Jerusalem.

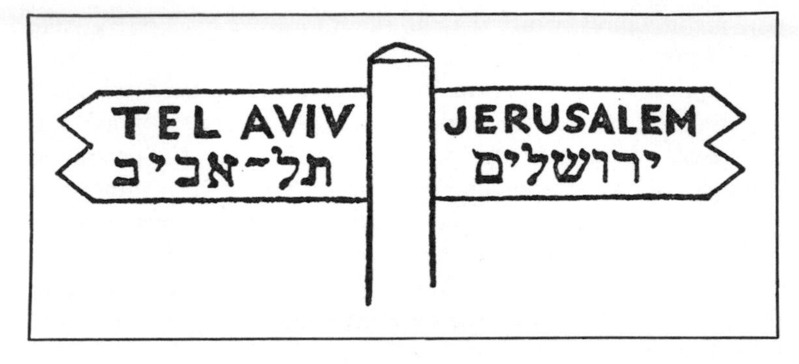

Jerusalem is one of the most ancient cities in the world; Tel Aviv is perhaps the most recent. At the beginning of this century, Tel Aviv was a desolate waste of sand. Jerusalem was already an ancient city of renown when King David captured it in 1000 B.C. The building of Tel Aviv began in 1909; Jerusalem was destroyed by Nebuchadnezzar, king of Babylon, in 587 B.C. Jerusalem is beautiful; Tel Aviv is ugly. Jerusalem is dignified and sacred; Tel Aviv is noisy and commercial. Tel Aviv is bursting with activity; Jerusalem is half dead. Tel Aviv is dedicated to a great and promising future; Jerusalem is the monument of a magnificent past. Tel Aviv is an American town; Jerusalem is much more European and yet Oriental at the same time. Jerusalem is the capital of Christianity, Judaism, and Islam; Tel Aviv is the real capital of Israel.

•

In Tel Aviv, the Israeli's home is not his castle. In too many instances, the Englishman's home is not the Englishman's castle either; it is the Englishman's prison. He does not lack privacy; he has too much of it. In Tel Aviv, the position is reversed. Tel Aviv is a clean, healthy, modern, ugly town, full of square-shaped, concrete buildings with useful balconies and bathrooms fitted with showers; and the house-proud wives keep all this admirably and spotlessly clean. And yet, one must admit that, in every dirty little Arab village, the mosque has more charm and architectural beauty than all the impressive mass of concrete in Tel Aviv put together.

People practically live on the balconies. Here they can listen—often, indeed, cannot help listening—to their neighbors' conversations. When you play bridge on the balcony, the people on the floor above or immediately opposite take a keen interest in your hand. Children playing in the street are in constant two-way communication with their parents several floors above. People listen to their neighbor's radio, and, when they have had enough, they just lean over into the next apartment and switch it off.

There is much noise in Tel Aviv, but it differs in quality from the London noise. In London, everybody is quiet; people do not talk; cars do not hoot; news vendors do not shout; and the cumulative effect of all this silence is the pandemonium of a huge metropolis. Tel Aviv's noise is the result of individual effort. Everybody does his best. Every throat, car horn, truck engine, radio, street peddler, angry truck-driver, anxious mamma, and obedient child makes its, his, or her contribution.

The people of Tel Aviv are constantly in a hurry. They rush about in their khaki shorts and shirts, carrying large, heavy briefcases, and are contemptuously called *schwitzers* by the people of Jerusalem. They buy newspapers and often stop for a *gazoz*—this being the national drink of Israel. It is fizzy water with fruit juice—orange, raspberry, pineapple, grapefruit, etc. Millions of gallons of *gozoz* are consumed in Tel Aviv—and very little alcohol. There is a current joke about a Christian and a Jew who get lost in the desert. They are found after many days of search and, when, at last, the rescue party arrives, they hear the Christian shout: "Water! Water!" and the Jew: "*Gazoz! Gazoz!*"

But all this hubbub is the beat of the city's life. People work very hard, and it would be rather unfair to smile at them just because work, according to our conception, is some vague activity engaged in between frequent cups of tea. On the whole, they are very pleasant-looking people in their khaki uniforms,

clean, freshly shaven, and tanned by the Mediterranean sun. You see few beggars in Tel Aviv; I personally saw none.

I saw, however, plenty of them in Jerusalem, where old Jewish gentlemen with long white beards, looking like ancient prophets —and some must be prophets by trade—approach you and ask for a little cash. If you give them a piastre or two, they bless you in enthusiastic and eloquent language; if you refuse them alms, they mutter a few words in Yiddish, and I always had the uncomfortable feeling that they were committing me to eternal damnation in the Jewish section of hell. I am not superstitious, but I dislike being damned by venerable prophets more than three times a day, so I decided to purchase eternal happiness at the price of a few grusch. When I found, however, that my salvation, even at the low estimate of two cents per prophet, would cost me a considerable sum in earthly cash, I took, I am afraid, unreasonable risks.

The first Jews who went to Palestine settled in Jerusalem. They were not Zionists. They were religious zealots who wanted to die in the city of the Temple. In due course, they died, but their spiritual inheritance is still alive. Their children and their children's children fill the streets—pale youths in *kaftans*, with side curls and a timid, troubled look in their eyes—in sharp contrast to the gay and healthy children of latter-day Israel. This older generation of Jews insisted on living in a ghetto, so it established its own, free ghetto in Jerusalem. It is strictly private. They do not wish to mix with the godless Jews in the khaki shorts. The gates of the ghetto are defended from within. How right my wife was when she remarked: "This must be the Jewish quarter of Jerusalem."

You see a large number of priests, too, clean-shaven monks with tight lips; Orthodox priests with long, black, spade beards; Anglican pastors; and thin and fat nuns from many world-famous convents.

The tempo of life is slow. No one hurries. The City, the nearby Wailing Wall, and the Tomb of King David are silent reminders to the inhabitants that a few hours, indeed, a few centuries, count for nothing.

•

For the history of Jerusalem and Tel Aviv, see some more learned books; on the problems of the armistice and internationalization, see the daily press; and, for a description of the streets and individual buildings, see Steimatzky's *Palestine Guide*. I have only attempted to give a general impression of the atmosphere of the two cities. Let me add one further observation which must strike any visitor and which may throw some additional light on the riddle why the British and the Jews could not get along well together. Some people say that the Jews were not picturesque enough for the British. As a friend of mine bitterly remarked in Tel Aviv: "If we had been riding on donkeys, wearing colorful prayer shawls, and uttering martial cries in Yiddish, I'm sure they'd have liked us more." Others say that the Jews were not native enough. Instead of taking orders in abject silence from their rulers, they argued and claimed their rights. Both theories may contain a particle of truth. I believe that I, too, may make some contribution to solving the problem. The sacred animal of the modern British, as of the ancient Egyptians, is the cat. Now, Israeli cats are not only few and far between, not only rather unpopular with the people, but also extremely ugly. They look like a cross between a miniature hyena and a gigantic rat. I do not suggest that the British disliked the Jews because the Jews disliked cats or that they like Arabs because Egyptians used to hold cats sacred. But I do suggest that the Approach to the Cat is a dividing line between peoples and civilizations. The Jews think the English love for cats hypocritical and silly. The English, on the other hand, are apt to think that people who do not love cats cannot be decent people. If they looked at the monstrous Jewish cats and thought that people have the kind of cats they deserve—well, then, it is just too obvious that the Mandate could not work.

7

BRITAIN
FRANCE
ITALY
GERMANY
SWITZERLAND
ISRAEL
√ JAPAN

FROM SIKLOS TO TOKYO

I was born in Siklos, Hungary.

Siklos is a small, sleepy, and dusty village, but, for the first ten years of my life, it was for me a magnificent place and the hub of intellectual life. After all, Siklos had 3,000 inhabitants—a veritable metropolis compared to, say, the neighboring Kisharsany, with its few hundred souls; Siklos was the so-called chief locality of a district, with various government offices, a tax office, a district court, two hotels, and even a bank; and we had policemen, not gendarmes—the truest token of urbanity and adulthood. And, then, Siklos people were so immensely superior. It is difficult to say which they despised more, the peasants of the surrounding villages or the inhabitants of Pécs, a largish town nearby. It was ridiculous and backward to be a villager, and it was effeminate and smug to be a town dweller. Siklos was just right. Mind you, it was not enough to come and settle in Siklos; you had to be a native of the place. Although there was one slight blot on my ancestry, since my mother had only married into Siklos society—she had come from Budapest—I still passed muster, since even my paternal great-grandfather had been born in Siklos. I belonged, in fact, to the salt of the earth.

I did not know then that the people of the surrounding villages, as well as the people of Pécs, thought just as poorly of us as we thought of them. My pride in Siklos and my local patriotism were boundless. Our local football team fought violent battles with those from the neighboring localities, especially Darda—another Siklos, not far away. The most renowned player of our team was a barber called Czinna. He came every day to shave my father, and my father grew much in my estimation because he was shaved by such an eminent person. I do not think that I have experienced a greater access of passion, a deeper emotional upheaval than I did at the Siklos–Darda football matches. And I do not remember many occasions in my life when I have been more downcast than on that dark day when Siklos was defeated by Darda, three goals to one.

When I was about four, we had to move to Pécs. This was in World War I, and the army unit which my father served was quartered at Pécs. I was never converted to Pécs. I kept a stiff upper lip; I endured the comforts and blessings of an easier and better life; I tried not to show my contempt for the city dwellers—too effeminate and smug, if you asked me—and I remained a true Siklos boy at heart.

At the end of the war, Siklos (we had returned by that time) was occupied by Yugoslav troops, and the place was about to be incorporated in the newly born state of Yugoslavia. At school, we were taught that the Serbian who had touched off the war by killing the crown prince of the Austro-Hungarian Empire was a true hero, that Hungary had been on the wrong side, and that Serbia had been on the right. Then Siklos was given back to Hungary, and we were told that the Serbian who had killed the crown prince was a base assassin and that Hungary was right in every respect, whereas Yugoslavia—and everybody, for that matter, with the single exception of Hungary—was wrong. Naturally, I instinctively sympathized with Hungary and became a staunch irredentist at the age of six or so.

Later, in Budapest, to which city we moved after the death of my father when I was ten, some subversive older friends assured me that irredentism was wrong; that Hungary had been guilty in her treatment of her national minorities, the Rumanians, Slovaks, and Croats; and that the Treaty of Trianon served her right. (When I began to think for myself, I realized that Hungary had indeed behaved badly toward her minorities; yet I remained convinced that the Treaty of Trianon was stupid, unjust, and vindictive.)

In the meantime, I graduated from the village to the capital, and here the swing in my feelings was violent indeed. I came to adore Budapest, and I am, in a mild way, ashamed of my village origin to this day. I love cities and dislike the countryside; I prefer trolley-buses to daffodils and exhaust fumes to the scent of acacias. Why? Simply to prove to the world and myself that I am a true metropolitan and not a little village boy.

Having left my village, I went on to leave my country, too. First, it was a temporary absence, a journalistic job to be done in London, but later it became clear that this temporary arrangement was to last all my life. Suddenly I found myself a foreigner —a stranger who stuttered in a peculiar semi-Asian tongue, who wore too long an overcoat, clicked his heels and bowed and, when asked, "How d'you do?" explained in detail how he was. The English laughed at me. But, in my eyes, London and Britain, with all their pride and self-assurance and conviction that they were the finest place on earth, were only a gigantic Siklos, and so I, too, laughed at them.

In London, I also discovered that I was a white man. I had never realized that before. Once, during World War II, I invited a Negro friend to supper. He nearly wept. He told me that, though people were often kind to him, I was the first white man to invite him into his home. It was most embarrassing. I did not mean it that way. I told him that, being a Central European, I was not all that white. I had my darkish spots in the eyes of the real master race. But he went on shedding his tears of gratitude. However, the one who never turned up for supper and never bothered to explain or apologize, before or since, was my grateful Negro friend.

It was in New York, after the war, that I first discovered that I was a European, too. There I learned to love Europe; I found I belonged to Europe; I was even perhaps proud of good old Europe. There is no place in the world where you can feel like a better and prouder European than in the United States of America.

Having been a proud villager of Siklos, a Hungarian patriot, a lover of Budapest, a lover of London, a British patriot, a foreigner, a white man, and a European, I set out on my journey to Asia. There my mind was invaded by a vague notion that I was really only a member of the human race. I am still not quite sure of this; things are not quite so simple as plausible slogans and catchwords would have us believe. But this may well be the truth. Now, when we have recently celebrated the centenary of Darwin's *Origin of Species*, on the one hand, and make effective preparations to blow up our planet, on the other, we may be slowly driven to the conclusion that the difference between white, brown, and black men is more accidental, more environmental, and much slighter than the difference between, say, cocker spaniels and Irish water spaniels and that there are, after all, more things to unite than to divide humanity. This, however, sounds a little far-fetched at present.

Nevertheless, my acquaintance with Asia reaffirmed the two main lessons of my younger days:

(1) I often thought of my Negro friend and was often reminded of the moral I had learned through him, namely, that though he always deserves our sympathy, THE VICTIM IS NOT ALWAYS RIGHT.

(2) And, seeing the pride and self-assurance of countries and peoples, their conviction that they had just the right amount

of sagacity, experience, and intelligence, as well as the happiest mixture of Western technical skill and Oriental wisdom, that they were all Chosen People with a glorious past and even more glorious future in store for them—in short, when I realized that they all regarded themselves as the Salt of the Earth, I realized that THE WHOLE WORLD IS ONE ENORMOUS SIKLOS.

THE FIRST MYSTERY

When I landed at Haneda airport, near Tokyo, in the company of some seventy other writers of various nationalities who had all come to take part in the International PEN Club Congress, I was stopped on the runway by a Japanese reporter.

"What are your impressions of Japan?" he asked me in hesitant but intelligible English and held notebook and pencil in readiness to jot down my reply.

Since we had to wait for the customs anyway, I summed up my impressions of my first three minutes on Japanese soil in a concise little talk lasting about a quarter of an hour.

I finished my discourse, and the reporter bowed to me; I

bowed in return. When he had departed, I turned to an old Japanese friend, whom I shall call Tanaka. He had spent years in England and was now meeting me at the airport.

"I hope he won't take it all seriously."

"He would take it very seriously," Tanaka replied. "But you needn't worry. The man didn't understand a word you said. He doesn't speak English."

"But he spoke to me . . . ," I protested.

"He knows a few odd words, but he doesn't understand it at all," Tanaka repeated firmly. "Apparently the office couldn't spare a man who really knows English."

"I see," I nodded. "This one was just getting in some practice."

Tanaka shook his head sadly. "Oh no, it's not that at all. They certainly would not do a discourteous thing like that. They are really very keen to know what your impressions of Japan are."

"They are keen?" I asked him, reflectively.

"Very keen indeed," said Tanaka earnestly.

I shrugged my shoulders. Well, I was in the mysterious Orient.

MANNERS

Before your first hour in Japan is over, you will have realized that you are among exquisitely well-mannered people. It is not a veneer; it is intrinsic and inbred in a people who take all their moral obligations seriously and who live on an overcrowded island. When you have as little space to yourself as the average Japanese, you must respect other people's privacy. Take, for example, the public telephone in the street. It is simply placed on some street vendor's counter—no booth or kiosk—and any passer-by could listen in to your most intimate conversations. But no one does. A man's telephone receiver is his castle.

And, also within the first hour, you will notice that people keep bowing to you. So you keep bowing to them. But you bow too deeply or not deeply enough; you bow to the wrong man at the wrong time; you do not clasp your hands in front of you, which is bad; or you do, which is worse. Then you notice that every grocery clerk bows with more grace and poise than any lady-in-waiting in a European court. Later still, you discover that the Japanese have a complicated hierarchy in bowing, which you may try to understand, but in vain. Who bows to whom? The basic rules inside the family are these: "The wife bows to the husband" (writes Ruth Benedict in *The Chrysanthemum and the Sword**), "the child bows to his father, younger brothers to elder brothers, the sister bows to all brothers of whatever age."

There are many kinds of bow. If you are sitting on the floor, Japanese fashion, you lean forward and touch the ground with your forehead, or else you nod. There are many intermediate varieties between these two. When bowing, you must watch the other fellow from the corner of your eye and remain in a bowing position as long as he does. You must not rise before him; he will not rise before you. Inexperienced bowers stay in a bent position for hours. In the old days, it was a habit of the Japanese to bow after every few words. The days of those exaggerated formalities are over. Nowadays, it is quite sufficient to bow at the end of each sentence, that is, at every full stop; a nod is enough at semicolons.

In bygone days, too, when you were riding in a vehicle and met a man to whom respect was due—which means anyone at all—you were expected to get out of the vehicle and bow to him. Today, it is not absolutely essential to stop your taxi and bow to all your acquaintances, but it is advisable to do it every now and then to show that you have some manners. About a dozen times during a journey should be ample.

Here are a few more elementary rules of Japanese etiquette. Nothing too advanced, only those absolutely essential ones which may help to prevent a European from seeming rude or making a fool of himself.

* New York: Houghton, Mifflin, 1947.

On leaving the Japanese house in which you are staying, you always have to declare, *Itte mairimasu* ("I am going now"), and on returning say, *Tadaima* ("I am just back"). To say on arrival that you are just leaving or on leaving that you have just come back is considered misleading.

If you are invited into a Japanese home, take off your shoes before stepping on the *tatami,* or floor mat. You will find two kinds of doors in a Japanese house; both are sliding doors. Whenever you open or close a sliding door, you have to kneel down. Having spent a good deal of time on your knees, you may sit down on the floor. (The almost complete absence of furniture in Japanese houses is a brilliant idea; space may be much better utilized, and furnishing is incomparably simpler and cheaper if it does not involve buying any furniture.) You sit on the floor or, rather, on your own legs; you are allowed a cushion; and your body should lean forward. A man's hands should be placed on his thighs; a woman's, clasped in front of her. A man's hands must never be placed on a woman's thighs. Should anyone enter the room, you remove yourself from the cushion onto the *tatami.* When the introductions are over, you move back onto the cushion.

Now, it may happen that you want to pass in front of a sitting person. Do not hesitate; it is perfectly simple. All you have to remember is that you remain on your knees, crawl along, and drag both your knees behind you at the same time. Anyone who moves his knees separately is regarded as a lout, fit only for the pigsty.

Then tea will be served. It is very bad manners not to sip it noisily. It shows a lack of appreciation. If a Japanese child sips his tea (or soup) quietly, he is told off by his mother. If you are offered more biscuits than you can encompass, you refuse by saying that you have had enough. Then your hostess will wrap them up for you, and you take them home. On departing, you leave the slippers you had to put on when entering the house at the door, facing inward, ready for the next visitor to step into.

The giving and the receiving of gifts have, as everyone

knows, their strict rules. The choice of wrapping paper for gifts is of the utmost importance. These rules are a little complicated, and it is quite enough if the foreign visitor gets acquainted with *dashi, hosho, torinoko, sugiwaragami, nishinouchi, noriire, minogami,* and *hanshi.* But these are the bare minima. The method of wrapping is also of decisive importance. I quote from *Japanese Etiquette: An Introduction.**

> Wrinkling must be avoided and the folding should be precise. Ordinarily the paper is wrapped so that the last fold comes on top of the package at the right-hand edge with the end of the paper extending all the way to the left-hand edge of the package. For unhappy occasions, however, the wrapping is reversed, with the last fold on the top of the package at the left-hand edge and the end of the paper extending all the way to the right-hand edge of the package. One must be very careful about how the paper is folded, for people are very sensitive about it. . . . Gifts with a red-and-white cord should be tied so that the red cord is on the right; and when using the gold-and-silver cord, the gold should be on the right.

At this point, I must admit, I interrupted my studies and decided to remain a lout, fit only for the pigsty.

SAMURAI AND POSTMEN

Once upon a time, I came to live in certain islands, called the British Isles, which lie off the shores of a great continent. When I went to explore certain other islands, called Japan, off the shores of another great continent, I was curious to see whether there was any similarity between the two peoples. One had heard so much of the "Prussians of the East" that one wanted to find out a little about the "British of the East" (be-

* *Japanese Etiquette: An Introduction* (Tokyo: World Fellowship Committee of the YMCA).

fore settling down to study the Japanese of the East). There must be some similarities between the Japanese and the British, I thought; after all, environment must have had some effect. And, indeed, we do not have far to seek. Certain parallels are so obvious that we need not dwell on them. Both nations are maritime nations, with long traditions and intimate ties with the sea; both are the most highly industrialized countries of their respective continents; and both hit on the obvious idea (obvious to sailors) of founding an empire and trying to rule the world. Both peoples have excellent manners; are disciplined in their own, different ways; and are able to think in global terms and in centuries—an attitude quite alien to land animals.

I have found, I think, the point where the Japanese differ most from the English and also the point where they almost improve on them, where the Japanese are more English than the English.

I was first of all put out to find that the "Oriental imperturbability" of the Japanese is an illusion and a myth. They are imperturbable enough as long as they are not properly roused. But, when roused, they are able to fly into the most spectacular rages, and the consequences are unpredictable. I have collected countless examples of what ought to be called "Oriental perturbability." It can be shattering enough even on the domestic scale. An English friend of mine, a bachelor, once asked his Japanese housekeeper to fetch some salt. This seemingly trivial request set off a terrific explosion. The girl wept and lamented vociferously for an hour and a half, her complaint being that, by asking for the salt, her employer had been rude enough to point out that she had forgotten it. At the climax of her paroxysm, she stormed out of the house, still in a state of uncontrollable fury. Two hours later, she returned as calm as an angel and courteous as a geisha. The whole matter would never have been mentioned again had not my friend, five months later, been foolish enough to ask where his shoes were, since he could not find them.

One of Japan's great literary works is *The Forty-Seven Ronins*, a tenth-century novel of romantic love and adventure. The story has been read by millions throughout the ages; it has been turned into a Kabuki play and is being made into a film. A retainer at the imperial court, anxious to humiliate a rival, advises the latter to wear the wrong pair of trousers for a ceremonial occasion. The warrior's humiliation is unutterable, and it demands a terrible vengeance. The story itself is really the history of this vengeance—the story of forty-seven brave, avenging samurai. All forty-seven are killed before this terrible tale is concluded; villages are burned and pillaged; countless people are ambushed, tortured, massacred; wives sell themselves to brothels to enable their husbands to carry on the fight; etc., etc. It is all very admirable and heroic. And it is all because of the wrong pair of trousers. On a similar occasion, in tenth-century Britain, when Sir Adalbert was similarly maliciously advised in the matter of trousers and deeply humiliated when he appeared unfittingly attired at King Edred's Court, he simply went home and changed his trousers. And thus we were deprived of an early masterpiece of English literature.

The point where the Japanese outdo the English in Englishness with flying colors, is in the muddle of their streets, or, rather, their postal addresses. London has achieved great and glorious results in these fields; yet, London is simply nowhere compared to Tokyo. Giving silly names to streets, roads, gardens, crescents, mews, walks, alleys, etc., and allocating numbers to houses in a haphazard and whimsical manner is quite a good line, but it is rather amateurish. It falls miles below Japanese standards. The Japanese have hit on the simple and logical idea that, if you really want muddle and chaos in your towns, you must give no names at all to your streets and no numbers to your houses; and, if you do occasionally provide names and numbers, it should be done only to give a false lead and increase the muddle. A postman may have a letter for, say, Shinkichi Vyeda San (*San* stands for Mr., Mrs., *or* Miss, which is helpful for the postman). People in the neighborhood may or may not have heard of him or her; they may or may not be able to tell the postman whether Vyeda San is a boy of four or a lady of eighty-seven; they may even be able to tell the postman where Mr. Vyeda—if he is a Mr.—lives, and eventually the postman may or may not find him; and Mr. Vyeda himself may, if found, come into an unclaimed inheritance of 124,000,000 yen. Or, again, he may not.

Nervous breakdown is a regular occupational disease of Japanese postmen after four years of service. There is a special hospital for nervous disorders which is reserved for postmen only; scores of people amble about with envelopes in their hands, vacant looks in their eyes. Their lips hardly moving, they mumble addresses like "*Shibuya-ku . . . Shibuya-ku . . .*" until the day when death relieves them.

A CLUE TO THE SECRET

The random observations of one's first few days may provide a clue to a question which is always lurking at the back of one's mind. And, if you tend to forget this question, a large number of the Britons and Americans you meet all over Asia—and in Europe and America, for that matter—will soon remind you of it. "It is all very interesting," they will say, "what you tell me about the Japanese and their charming ways and many talents and all that sort of thing. But I never want to see another Japanese in my life if I can help it. For me, they have entirely different associations—not exactly charm and pleasantness." This is, of course, the voice of the former prisoner of war or civilian internee in Japanese hands. Do not argue with them; they have very good reasons for saying all this.

What is the truth? Where shall we seek a clue to the secret?

First of all, I think, one has to remember that the Japanese are perhaps the one nation in the world which is itself seeking a clue to a secret. They want to find the magic word opening up national success; they are searching for the Miraculous Signpost leading to the Righ Road, for the Secret Key that opens the Gates of Wisdom and Abundance. Until the arrival of Commodore Perry, they believed that Splendid Isolation was the magic phrase (what an odd, Oriental idea, if one comes to think of it). Then they found a more-or-less satisfying answer in Industrialization. Nevertheless, Industrialization turned out not to be the full answer, and they tried to supplement it with fascism.

It is a peculiar, Japanese kind of fascism—tyranny without a tyrant. Japan has always been ruled by a class or a clique, never by a single dictator. They also had a deity—the emperor—who was revered but not obeyed, who was prayed to like a wooden idol but was not supposed to announce his own wishes any more than a wooden idol. When, in the end, he did speak—and I shall describe the occasion presently—his words were obeyed with the devotion due a miraculous happening. Indeed, he was followed with the blind devotion due a wooden idol or to a real god.

The magic of fascism was wiped out simply because it did not work. It did not lead to salvation; it led to destruction and humiliation. So the other recipe—the formula of the victors, called democracy—had to be tried. And the Japanese are still trying it.

Are they sincere in this? The question of sincerity does not come into it at all. If, when you are experimenting in a laboratory, one given mixture does not work, you try another; you substitute, say, the sulpho group for the nitro group to see whether certain results ensue. Faith and sincerity have nothing to do with it. You make your experiment and await the result, perhaps with anticipation, even excitement, but always with a degree of scientific detachment.

Industrialization did work, so the Japanese have stuck to it; should democracy work, they will stick to it, too. If not, not.

WOMEN

If you want to be a Japanese, be a man. It is a man's country, and it is the women who make it a man's country.

When, after your first days in Japan, you have taken note of all the obvious and conspicuous, but nonetheless fascinating, eccentricities and you try to look a little under the surface, a conviction will start growing in your mind that Japan is a country with a split personality. It is not a single split; there is a treble split, cutting in various directions and on various planes. A split was caused in this country of the invincible by Japan's defeat in 1945, the first in her history; there is another wide split between the younger and the older generation; and, third, between the old-fashioned and the modern woman.

These divisions are not clear-cut; no division is ever clear-cut; divisions are not very helpful in this respect. The confusing habit of divisions is responsible for a great deal of muddle in our world.

Some people will try to convince you that the Japanese women's liberation movement, far from being a general revolt of the younger generation, is simply a revolt of the women of Tokyo and a few other large cities. The vast countryside, they say, goes on in the same old way, unperturbed. This is not true; the capital and some large cities may have been the center of this social earthquake, but the tremors were and are being felt all over the country. It is true, however, that not all the young women are in the fight. Some of them would like to remain slaves—just as in America in the last century many Negroes fought for slavery and just as many butlers in Britain insist on voting for the Tories.

This split mind clearly manifests itself in the effect of dress on the Japanese personality. Millions of Japanese wear kimonos at home (men included, of course) and Western dress out of doors on most but not all occasions. In Western dress, the couple walk abreast, the husband is polite if not deferential to his wife and opens doors for her. But, as soon as he puts his kimono on, he becomes the domestic potentate again. He walks in front of his wife; he would not dream of getting, say, a newspaper for himself, but orders his wife to fetch it for him. In the kimono, he is the lord and master. And, when he takes his kimono off for the family bath—in simpler households, where they have one tub only, people take their baths in turn—there is no question but that the master of the house should have the first bath.

For the old-fashioned Japanese woman, life is perpetual drudgery. Household work is heavier for her than for her European or American sister. There is less furniture in the house, it is true, but putting away the whole bed or mat every morning and bringing it out again at night is, I am told, heavier work than making the bed in European fashion. Cooking, too, means more fiddling work in antiquated kitchens, and the innumerable tiny dishes they use do not turn the washing into a quick and pleasant pastime either. An American husband may (or must) help his wife with the dish-washing; in Japan, this sounds like an incredible joke, invented by anti-American slanderers. (By the way, the gulf between the patriarchal Japanese outlook and the matriarchal American outlook has been one of the most significant factors which destine these two peoples to remain strangers.)

Shopping is the only household duty which is easier for at least the middle-class Japanese woman than it is in the West. Everything is delivered to her home. Boys on bicycles keep arriving and ringing her bell twenty or thirty times every morning, each of them bringing one item—bread, coffee, tea, rice, meat, fish, vegetables, wine, oranges, the laundry, flowers, etc. The poorer women, however, go out to do the shopping themselves. Delivery does not cost anything extra, but these women dislike the idea of having to show their seedy and humble homes to tradesmen.

There is one duty of which the Japanese women are almost completely acquitted—entertainment in the home. The Japanese regard it as impolite and insufficiently formal to entertain guests at home, so they take them to restaurants and geisha houses, and the wives stay at home. (I shall have more to say later about the strong connection between the sexual and the commercial life of the Japanese.) The home is often poor and needy; the geisha house is a place of elegance and splendor.

Injustice, as always, breeds further injustice. Owing to this tradition, the Japanese man associates glamor, happiness, and the beauties of life with being away from his home; he associates only poverty, drabness, and worries with his wife.

It is often alleged that Japanese women do not really mind when their husbands spend nights with other women and keep up permanent connections with geishas or other ladies of easy virtue. They do mind, of course, but until recently they could do nothing about it. In most cases, the men do not even bother to hide their adventures from their wives; there is no secrecy about visiting prostitutes. Divorces are few and far between (well below 20,000 a year in the whole country), nevertheless, they are possible, but the husband's adultery is not legal ground for divorce.

What about adultery by the wife? The problem does not arise. The Japanese are proud to emphasize that their women are the most faithful in the world. This is true. The reason for this is the shining virtue of Japanese women, slightly enhanced by a complete lack of opportunity.

If the poorer woman's life is perpetual drudgery, the richer woman's life is complete boredom. They have servants who do all the chores for them, and, consequently, they have nothing to do but go with other bored ladies to the Kabuki or watch baseball. But you cannot always go to the Kabuki or watch baseball. So they sit at home and grow fat. Not that they all grow fat; indeed, nowhere in the world have I seen so many exquisitely beautiful women as in Japan.

Even so, the old-fashioned woman is not the withering, broken flower one would imagine. She is, more often than not, a pretty formidable personality, with a great deal to say about her children's education and marriage and also about money matters. And she says what she has to say pretty distinctly. She is not only a slave in the background; she is also a tyrant in the background.

It was against this situation that the younger generation rebelled so forcefully. The Americans have liberated at least the women of Japan or have given them the chance of liberating themselves. Today, women have the vote; they study at the universities; they take jobs; and fewer and fewer marriages are arranged by the parents without consulting the young people concerned (although this is still the general rule in Japan). Many women are determined fighters for equality. But fighting for equality is definitely an outdoor activity. When the brave suffragette arrives home and puts on her kimono, she will still leap to her feet and make a dash for the newspaper as soon as her husband snaps his fingers.

THE GEISHA

Europeans of both sexes seem to be under the impression that the geisha girl is a kind of superior prostitute. But most European husbands (which category, I repeat, includes Americans), on their return from Japan, are at pains to explain that the geisha girls are not prostitutes at all. Nothing could be further from the truth; they are highly cultivated young ladies with exquisite manners; they are dancers, singers, and entertainers of talent; and it is not on their skill in the art of love but on their wit and repartee that their reputation rests.

The truth is that the geisha girl is a cultured, charming, and highly trained young prostitute with a gift for repartee. As far as the repartee is concerned, I spent one evening in the company of a geisha and got much more repartee than I had bargained for. As soon as the young lady, who wore a beautiful kimono and a very elaborate hairstyle, discovered, after a few dozen respectful bows on her part, that I was treating her as an equal, she ceased to stand on ceremony with me and became as sassy (though endearingly sassy) as any spirited European schoolgirl. She made faces at me and dug me in the ribs, and, whenever she noticed that my squatting technique did not come up to scratch, she would give me a push, so that I lost my balance and rolled over.

It is quite true, nevertheless, that, though all geishas can be bought for the night (it is a matter of price, and a very high price at that), a geisha party, much more often than not, means only supper, drinking sake, watching dancing and listening to singing, and gay conversation (full of repartee). *Mamasan* is not surprised if someone wishes to linger late in one of those tiny little Japanese houses where the parties take place, but, as a rule, after midnight the guests return to their family hearths.

At the base of all this expensive and ritualistic entertainment lies an ancient Oriental tradition called the Expense Account. Any attempt at explaining to my readers what is meant by an Expense Account would take us too far afield. Suffice it to say that it became popular in Japan well after the Meiji Restoration, in fact, in the MacArthur era. And, when I say "popular," I am not using the word injudiciously. In no country in the world are sex life and big business so interdependent as in Japan. No contract worthy of the name has ever been signed anywhere other than in a geisha house. If you want to do business, you have to throw a geisha party. No geisha party, no business. And that's that.

A young German who had been living in Tokyo for about four years and was on the way to making a business career for himself, talked to me on this subject.

"I am talking to you man to man," he said. "Please don't give me away; it would make me ridiculous. I would lose face. Promise?"

I promised.

He looked around cautiously and then went on:

"I love my wife. She is a Japanese girl. I have never been unfaithful to her and do not intend to be. All the same, I have to spend at least three nights a week in brothels. Very well, call them geisha houses. I call them brothels. I slip away at midnight all right as, in fact, many of my Japanese business acquaintances do, too. It's not so bad when you can slip out. But I can't get out of going to the parties. How would you like to go to brothels three times a week?"

I did not reply to this question; if seemed much too personal.

"My wife does not suspect me of being faithful to her," he went on. "That's my shady secret. She would think rather poorly of me if she found out. You won't talk? You promised. . . ."

I told him not to worry.

"The other day, I thought I had tricked three Japanese," he said with a wide grin. "I produced the contracts from my desk out of the blue and handed them a pen. All this was in my office, mind you. They were so taken aback and embarrassed that they signed. After they'd gone, I felt pretty elated. 'No geishas for me tonight,' I thought, rubbing my hands with satisfaction. But I laughed too soon. That evening, the three Japanese gentlemen, all smiles and bows, reappeared in my office. They did not explain why they had come. They didn't need to. Off we went to the bro . . . I mean to one of those houses of traditional geisha entertainment."

•

The geishas are the aristocracy of an old profession. No clan, however, consists of an aristocracy only. Tokyo, I believe, has almost as many streetwalkers as London. And then there are the brothels, proper and undisguised. Yoshiwara alone employs about a thousand girls in its three hundred establishments. Then there are the "on-limit" night clubs (meaning that they were not out of bounds to American soldiers). The hostesses in these night clubs may be taken elsewhere if you pay the proprietor some compensation. One night, four of us—a married couple, a friend of mine, and I—ventured into an on-limit place. As soon as we sat down at a table, two hostesses appeared, bowed, and sat down next to my friend and me; as unaccompanied males, we were considered fair game. I did not say anything to the very attractive young lady who attached herself to me, but, after five minutes, I asked her for a dance. Considering the way I dance, this was not too kind of me. As soon as we could speak in private, she asked me in slow and precise English:

"Do you desire me?" These were the first words she uttered.

I was a little embarrassed; no woman had ever opened a conversation with me in this way before. But I have been a polite man all my life, so I told her that I did.

She bowed deeply.

Apparently it was very kind of me to desire her.

•

The Japanese are reported to be sexually more potent and active than any other race except the Negroes. I do not know whether this is true or merely self-advertisement. Nevertheless, a certain amount of evidence goes to suggest that this allegation has a great deal of truth in it. Yet, Tokyo is not a sexy place; it is not erotic; it is simply copulative.

Most people visit hotels for this purpose. All the hotels in Tokyo—with the exception of a few international ones—cater to this type of clientele quite openly; there is nothing illegal about it. They have price lists for one hour, two hours, etc. In addition, these hotels have their ordinary tourists and permanent residents, but they would not be able to live on them alone.

"There are about 20,000 hotels in Tokyo," a Japanese friend explained to me. "Say they all have at least ten rooms. They must hire these rooms out at least five times a day to make them pay. That means a million couples—two million people a day. And that's only in the hotels. Not counting the brothels at all. And all this in Tokyo alone."

THE EARTH SPIDER

Naturally, I went one day to the Kabuki theater; a visit to Japan without seeing Kabuki is like a visit to Paris without seeing the Louvre. The Kabuki program started at eleven o'clock in the morning with a seventh-century love-thriller involving Prince O-ama and Princess Nukada. There were three more plays before an hour's break for lunch. In the afternoon, it began all over again with a play called *Onna Shijin.* The hero of this was Gyo-Genki, a supremely beautiful woman and a great poet, the daughter of Gyo-bo, a "madman in a house of pleasure." Quite a promising start. The play itself lived up to our expectations.

Then came my own favorite, *The Earth Spider.* When the curtain rises, we see the orchestra squatting at the back of the stage (as in all Kabuki plays), amid very impressive and beautiful scenery. We see a nobleman by the name of Minamoto Yorimutsu. He has fallen ill and cannot understand what is wrong with him. People, by the way, do not speak in Kabuki plays. They chant in an artificial, monotonous, high-pitched voice; they also moan, mutter, groan, squeal, wail, whimper, whine, snivel, and roar. This is a very ancient tradition, and, if you start watching Kabuki plays at the age of two, you may get used to it. If you start later, you wonder.

Yorimutsu is visited by Kocho, a ravishingly beautiful lady-in-waiting, who dances for the sick man. The dance does not cure him. (It would have cured me, but that is not the point.) Kocho is followed by another visitor in the guise of a traveling priest. But he is not a traveling priest at all—far from it; he is the Earth Spider. From his mask, you can see immediately that he is not a sympathetic character. He walks in extremely slowly, roughly a quarter of a mile per hour. A number of other people—Yorimutsu's servants—sit, kneel, and squat about. Some people in the audience shriek with excitement. At last, the visitor throws a spider at Yorimutsu, who is, however, on the alert; he jumps up, snatches his sword, and slashes at the sham priest. The latter, however, vanishes into thin air. "Vanishing into thin air" is represented by his strolling away rather slowly and comfortably.

All the members of the Yorimutsu household now gather and decide that quick action must be taken. The Earth Spider must be sought out in his cave and killed. For about half an hour they chant and whine, "Let's follow him! Let's run after him! We mustn't give him a chance to run away." There is tremendous excitement, expressed by the fact that they all sit about quietly, almost motionless. They repeat: "Let us hurry! Let us gallop! We have not a moment to lose!" Whereupon they all go on sitting there.

The afternoon wears on. Suddenly, Yorimutsu shouts:

"Aa . . . !" (Emphasis on the second "a.") He stamps his foot twice. The chorus starts chanting again!

"Go, go and avenge yourself on the Earth Spider."

Yorimutsu gives his answer in whispers; he informs his household that he is in a frantic rage and that they must hurry desperately, otherwise the monster might get away. One cannot be quick enough in such matters. Then he declares, "Aa!" again and stamps his foot three times.

When I wake up about three quarters of an hour later, the chase is at its height. Three men are moving around the stage to declare about a dozen times that everything depends on speed; otherwise the monster might have a chance to escape. Then the pace of the chase quickens; the three men —still motionless—become more emphatic on this point and sit down to debate it. "Let us not spare ourselves! Who thinks of himself in such an hour as this? We have a sacred duty to perform."

A number of new pursuers now arrive, accompanied by a sort of gentle lullaby. They fully agree with the views of the three. "We cannot have a moment's rest until that curse, the Earth Spider, is slain." They sit down. A boy comes in moaning: "Let us pursue him!" He performs a dance with two flags. After the dance, the boy says, "Let us not waste a single moment," and dances another dance with seven fairies. The three original pursuers, still remarkably fresh, although they have been squatting on the floor for so long, shout as the boy dances: "Hurry, hurry! Not a moment is left!" The air is now so charged with urgency and tension that everyone sits down—the boy, the seven fairies, and all.

Thirteen other people rush in on their knees. They lie down and kick their legs in the air. They get up after a considerable time and dance, first, a doll dance, then a puppet dance, and, finally, a Japanese polka. When this is over, two men drag in a pedestal and leave it on the right side of the stage.

Someone starts knocking. The knocking goes on for twenty-three minutes. Another person chants, "Ooooooh . . ." with guitar accompaniment for thirty-four minutes. Then he says, "Ooooooh . . ." without the guitar for seventeen minutes. Then guitar without "Ooooooh . . ." for eighteen minutes.

The cave is pushed on with the monster inside. The pursuers reappear all dressed in yellow (I forgot to mention that they all went out during the "Ooooooh's"). One of them makes a brief (nine-minute) chanting speech on the theme, "We must not waste a minute, otherwise the monster might get away." They all squat, then get up, go out, and reappear in green. This time they tell us about the frightful and hair-raising fate that awaits the Earth Spider.

They surround the cave and look at the monster, but none of them sees him. The monster utters an awful and terrifying sound; no one hears him. The pursuers say: "We shall never find him. Our relentless pursuit was all in vain. The monster has managed to get away. Alas! All hope is now lost."

They dance around the cave. (They are in purple now.) Even the monster cannot bear to leave them in such deep despair any longer, so he comes out of the cave. At once, they all sit down. A great deal of chanting ensues; the monster prepares for the final life-and-death struggle. But no one offers combat; in fact, no one moves. Suddenly, the monster, the Earth Spider, collapses and dies. I think that he has had a stroke. Boredom may have brought it on.

The monster is dead. The pursuers dance around his corpse and congratulate one another on their bravery and resourcefulness.

There were two more Kabuki plays that evening—one about a mask-maker, the other about a young widower who still adored his deceased wife. These two last plays, however, lacked the liveliness and raciness of *The Earth Spider.*

THE FROG AND ETERNITY

I was about nine years old when I heard a certain old joke —old even when I was nine. I thought it very funny. A man is asked whether he can play the violin. "How should I know," he replies, "when I never tried it?"

I remember that I was, for a long time, intrigued by the possibility that I, too, might be a violin virtuoso. I felt that I ought to try, but have never done so to this day.

•

Many of my Japanese friends, as well as my Japanese publishers, gave me books of Japanese poetry translated into English. I had known something of Japanese poetry and its basic rules—the frequent alternation of five and seven syllables and a few other points—but, now that I was reading more of them than ever before in my life, these poems really started growing on me. Soon I could not resist the temptation of trying my own hand at this art. So I wrote a poem.

I am looking at a frog.
He smiles back at me.
Frogs' smiles always remind me of
Eternity.

Since this was definitely encouraging, I wrote another one after a few days' reflection:

I am looking at a frog.
He smiles back at me.
Frogs' smiles always remind me of
Snow.

And who can blame me for turning it into a trilogy?

A frog looks at me.
I am smiling back at him.
My smile always reminds frogs of
The Spring and the Moon.

Ah, the Moon. . . .

I showed my poems to some Japanese friends, who all declared that they were superb, verging on the great. They said this so convincingly that, for a while, I was not at all certain who was pulling whose leg. But, when my three poems were translated into Japanese and published in one of the leading poetry magazines, I became pensive and wistful.

I had known nothing of my power, simply because I had never tried to write Japanese poetry, just as I had never tried to play the violin. Is it possible—I ask my readers—is it possible that I am one of the greatest Japanese poets of this age?